FREE IND

2nd Edition 2023, paperback.
ISBN: 978-0-646-87328-2

FREE INDEED

REVISED EDITION 2023

AN AWAKENING TO TRUE IDENTITY AND THE REAL SUBSTANCE OF SALVATION

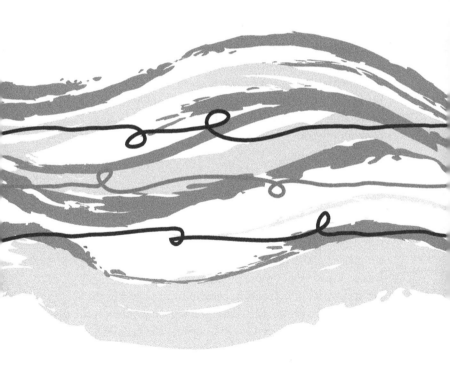

MANDY WOODHOUSE

My beautiful friend Mandy Woodhouse is not only a dear friend to me, but she is a friend of God. She is a powerful heralded of the Lord's truth and His heart. Her new book Free Indeed is full of deep truths and revelation that will not only catapult you further into your identity and destiny, but awaken you to the revelation of who you are in Christ. There is an impartation for healing and deliverance in these pages as you encounter our beautiful Jesus. This is a deep well of treasure that is life changing!

Lana Vawser
Lana Vawser Ministries
Lanavawser.com

Free Indeed is a book that you must read! Just the title of each chapter captivates you before you even read it. What a treasure Mandy has given to us. You can feel her heart and her love for Jesus in every word written. Thank you, Mandy, for your obedience to the Lord, I cannot wait to get this book for others!

Bill and Dana Turner
Cohosts of Your Morning Manna
WUCC999.com, South Carolina USA

It is very rare to pick up a book and be so persuaded of the author's careful care, love and concern for the reader. Free Indeed is just one of those little gems. Mandy's heart and her strong gift of mercy is so beautifully displayed in the pages of this treasure. Rich with personal encounters and experiences, Free Indeed is a journey into the believer's path to complete freedom through recognising their righteous identity in Christ. I truly loved the relational tone of this book. It really makes the material relatable and real. Any reader can pick it up and be invited into their own encounter with the love of God and the truth of who they really are.

Naomi Byers
Founder, Naomi Byers Ministries
Founder Nesher – Eagles Take Flight Prophetic Community

Mandy's bravery in sharing her personal journey of discovering the truth about her identity in Christ is both breathtaking and refreshing. Her deep vulnerability enables readers to instantly relate with her story and begin to understand their own righteousness. Free Indeed is a perfect balance of scripturally founded truth made tangible through personal testimony and revelation. This powerful combo makes it simple for readers to identify their own negative thought patterns or struggles and then translate the truths contained in this book directly to their own lives. The freedom ensuing this book will be countless, as sons and daughters realize the truth about who they are in Christ and live boldly from the place of their new creation identity.

Rachel McInnes
Church Planter
Associate Leader, Multiply Movement
Brisbane, Australia

Free Indeed is a genuine and refreshing gift! My friend Mandy Woodhouse has taken the dense and profound revelation of righteousness and sonship, and 'put legs on it' in this heartfelt project. Mandy speaks with an open-heartedness and carries a grace to make things relevant. She writes the way she lives and is having an impact on many. This book is filled with personal testimonies of a life lived and transformed by a powerful gospel, integrating the truth into real life and prophesying freedom for others. I know this book will help many to make sense of the practical ways in which the gospel can change our lives. I highly recommend this book and know it will bless many!

Mark Greenwood
Author of Awake to Righteousness

The writing of Mandy Woodhouse displays vibrant words of life that point readers to the goodness of God as their Heavenly Father. The transparency and from the heart approach she shows as a prophetic intercessor is refreshing!

Joel Yount
Co-founder of Spirit Fuel – A Prophetic Online Platform
www.spiritfuel.me

What powerful insights! Free Indeed beautifully weaves together a tapestry of God's Word, establishing a solid Biblical foundation with Mandy's journey and relentless pursuit for freedom, ultimately equipping every reader with practical tools to be free. Through the vulnerability shared in these pages, Mandy exposes countless "lies" that prevent many from finding freedom. God's transforming power is evident in Mandy's journey by those who are transformed around her. The keys found in this book will set many captives free and propel the global Church to destiny.

Christy Austin
Co-Founder Enkindle Ministries (USA)
Licensed Therapist

As you pour over these pages, you will find yourself drawn into a fresh invitation to unpack the mystery of who we are, as a new creation in Christ. Mandy's ability to convey this message with vulnerability and personal anecdotes, whilst rightly dividing scripture is a gift to the body, (both the young and mature believer). This book was an absolute joy to read, imparting undiluted truth with the grace to install revelation into the hands of the reader. The precision and conciseness within this remarkable writing, will instill a confidence to fully appropriate the finished work of the cross. I believe Free Indeed will be a catalyst to a renewed mind and a transformed life, a seed that will bear lasting fruit for future generations.

Jason Harrison
Senior Leader, New Nature Church
As He Is Ministries

Free Indeed is one of the most incredibly practical books on how to walk and live every day in freedom, the way Jesus intended it to be. Mandy opens up and expands on the deep but simplicity of our new nature in Christ. This book takes personal testimonies and truths and marries them together in beautiful harmony.

I would highly recommend this book and believe it will help many people of all works of life find faith and hope to live free indeed.

Liam Swaine
The Sanctuary Church
Senior Leader

Mandy knows Jesus. She knows His nature, His character, and His heart. She also knows what it's like to be bombarded by the lies of the enemy, such as, "I'm not good enough," "There's something wrong with me," "I'm a lost cause," etc. For many of us, these lies are all too real. But what if we could be truly free? Free Indeed is not a book full of fluffy anecdotes or suggestions to combat these lies. It is packed with hard-hitting biblical truths that expose the lies many of us have found ourselves in agreement with, replacing them with the truth. Mandy reveals that we do not have freedom dangling in front of us like a carrot on a string. When we say "yes" to Jesus, we are not just a little free, clinging to the promise of freedom on the other side of eternity. We are utterly free and transformed right now! We are confident that if you truly take the words in this book to heart, you will never be the same!

Jeff & Lauren Tharp
Hosts of ElijahFire

Table of Contents

Mandy's Note

This is my second release of Free Indeed. The first book came out in 2020, and as proud of it as I am, I feel like the past few years have given me greater understanding that I must not ignore. I have revised a few things, expounded on a few ideas, changed some things that He asked me to change and even added a chapter partially written by my amazing husband. I especially bring clarity, in this revision, around the idea of counseling, inner healing, and the fact that you can be free indeed and still need help sometimes.

As I said in my first release in 2020, I never would have seen myself writing a book on a topic like this. The topics of hope, joy, discernment or even prayer – absolutely (and I still may, most likely). But the idea of freedom...NEVER.

"It's too risky" is a thought that I have had time and time again regarding this book, even after the first release. But hey – Jesus asked us to do hard things with Him, did He not? And His fingerprints are all over these pages.

This revelation has changed my born-again life. I have witnessed such transformation in myself and the lives of those who really grasp this revelation that I am convinced that it is absolutely the GOOD NEWS. And good news must be shared.

I am still finding language and still asking for deeper revelation in the areas of freedom, but I believe that the thought processes and heavenly encounters that I have shared here have built a solid foundation for understanding a core message. If anything, it will indeed poke holes through any untruths that you may have engaged with! As a former primary and high school teacher, my teaching style is simple language and easy illustrations to make you think.

Jesus is so kind as to have given me most of these illustrations through supernatural encounters with Himself. To be completely candid, I believe that the encounters in this book are what sets it apart from other books of this nature. I love how the Father speaks to His children in unexplainable ways.

When writing my second manuscript, I felt the Lord say to me that though this little book may or may not be read across the nations, it will be put in the hands of several people who will change a part of the world, simply because of what has been awakened in them here, reading the words in this book.

In my humble opinion, *one single life walking in freedom and knowing Jesus more intimately is completely reason enough to release this book, time and time again.* In fact, I have been informed of at last three lives who came to know Jesus for the first time while reading the 2020 edition of this book!

He is so beautiful....

One thing to remember while reading is that friendship with God is *everything*. Abiding in His love is what keeps our hearts free, keeps us walking in love, and keeps us encouraged so as to not be hardened by the deceitfulness of sin (Hebrews 3:13).

A friend asked me awhile back what it is that I truly *burn for*. I have many gifts and passions, but I think what makes me the most alive and on fire is teaching people about JESUS. He is my absolute favorite subject. And truly, this book is all about HIM. I love that some of my readers are about to truly SEE themselves in truth for the first time, but I love even more that by reading this you can go deeper and grow more intimate with Jesus. Our righteousness would be nothing if not for Him, and He made us righteous so that we could find intimacy with Him. I pray that you keep this truth in mind as you read.

One final thing: The truth really IS this good. This revelation is a game-changer. But that is who Jesus is, right? He changes EVERYTHING. And without faith in Him, none of this would be possible.

Enjoy the journey as it unfolds.

The pages in this book are not made up
of long-winded theology text. This is a documented
journey, in simple and very personal language, that
highlights the fully transformed nature and identity of a
born-again Christian. It is also a prophetic declaration of
an awakening taking place in the Church to these truths,
and the roar across the earth of a bold lion who finally
knows who it is. This supernatural journey magnifies
Jesus, the One who made it all possible.
You were born again to be free.

Acknowledgements

Special thanks to the champion of my heart and my best friend, Carston Woodhouse, for the love, support and encouragement while I journeyed through this. My amazing Dad, James Marks, who has always supported me in every adventure I've had with the Lord. To Lori Boudreaux (my sister in every way except by blood), Tim & Rachel McInnes, Jason & Rachel Harrison, Bill & Dana Turner, The Mergard Family, Matt & Trish Beckenham, Liam Swaine, Naomi Byers, Jess Woodhouse and Josiah & Rachel Trigg for all their encouragement and love. To Daniel Zelli for taking the time to read through these pages at the very beginning and give such carefully thought-out feedback. Special thanks to my "Free Indeed" ladies from my first ever mentor group – you all know who you are. To my dear friend, Lana Vawser, who was the first person to push me to write something big! To Mark Greenwood for the endless processing and encouragement (and even the little "pushes"), the awesome coffees and for believing in me and in this book as you have. To Julia Lefik, who once again blew me away with her excellence in formatting the book. I love you all.

Finally, to my Jesus. My best friend. My Savior

and the Lord of my life. The one who made this book possible, and the one who has set me free. You are worthy of it all.

Foreword

When Mandy asked if we would write this foreword, we both jumped at the opportunity. Mandy and Carston carry such a love for people and a passion for them to know the love of God. They are champions of the Kingdom of God, as they are deep-hearted, and love helping people find their worth.

There has been an emphasis recently on the awakening of God's people to understand the freedom we have been designed to be living in. All around the world, we are hearing this message as it flows through God's people.

We believe we are living in a time when the New Wine Jesus spoke of is being released through His Bride. As He did in Acts, the Holy Spirit is making himself known through the lives and hearts of people all over the world. The Remnant is awakening. The Bride is forming in ways that are shedding the religious spirit and living from the freedom of the Holy Spirit.

You are invited to witness their experiences of discovering freedom: for Mandy through testimonies of life and her intimate relationship with God, and for Carston through his skill of clarifying scripture to reveal truth.

The uniqueness of this book is found in

Mandy's willingness to let us see the intimacy she has discovered in hearing Jesus speak to her. Year after year, Mandy has found the repeated and trusted message of Jesus' faithfulness and His desire to never leave her.

These words have flowed naturally from Mandy's life. Anyone who knows her, would automatically testify to the hope she carries and the pure faith she lives her life by. Mandy gives you her personal accounts of struggle and searching for her own freedom as encouragement. It's from this position that she invites you to join her on a journey to search for revelation and understanding about what it means for you to live free indeed.

As she testifies to events, dreams, and revelations she has received, she grounds each one in scripture and offers personal experiences. Through this, you will be invited to receive from the wealth of her heart as she generously shares her treasures.

In this re-release, Carston has added a chapter where he unfolds scripture to reveal the truths of Romans 7 in context with Romans 6 and 8. He skillfully unlocks the mystery and wonder of the grace and acceptance that undergirds Romans. You will be jumping for joy with the freedom you discover through this chapter as it adds to Mandy's testimonies. They work well together.

May the boldness of their hearts awaken parts of your spirit that have been slumbering, and may it reveal greater understanding of how you can live free indeed.

Matt & Trish Beckenham
Greater Things International

Introduction

And you will know the truth, and the truth will set you free. — John 8:32

The enemy has worked hard to stifle this message out of me and keep these words from going forth. Really hear what I am about to say: *The devil does NOT want you walking in freedom.* In fact, he would rather you live forever under the lie that you are not free at all, or that you never will be this side of Heaven. He loves seeing God's children bound up, shut up and living with aborted dreams.

The devil is rejected, without hope, without peace and incredibly angry so he will do whatever he can to taint the thinking of a born-again child of God, and thus contaminate our minds and behavior to be like his. If he can get you to not "pick up your cross and daily follow Him" (Luke 9:23) because you think you simply cannot do it because of the junk in your life, then he will pursue that old lie. If the devil can keep you from living fully surrendered to the Lordship of Jesus out of fear of "messing up" or "having too many issues," then he will push that agenda all day long. If he can get you distracted with consuming thoughts of how to "fix yourself" instead of just loving on the Father and letting Him love on you, then that will be his biggest tactic.

In fact, he has used those strategies on me most of my life. You see, the devil hates Jesus, and he therefore hates anything that looks like Jesus – and that, my friend, is me and it is YOU.

You read that right. YOU look like JESUS, if indeed the Spirit of God lives within you. *"By this is love perfected with us, so that we may have confidence for the day of judgment, **because as he is so also are we in this world** (1 John 4:17)."*

One of the biggest lies that the enemy throws at the Church is that she will never look like Jesus or walk in His complete freedom until we all enter Heaven's gates. Engaging this lie and believing it is actually what aids many believers into falling for the trap of ongoing sin, dark seasons of guilt-driven depression and even crippling anxiety. It keeps us from being rooted by living water and producing fruit in every season (Psalm 1). This lie even keeps us from being able to fully yield our lives to the supreme authority of Jesus (Lordship) because of how self-consumed we become. If a person partners with the lie that they will "never" be free, then they act out what they believe, which is a counterfeit identity. Counterfeit identities are what the enemy uses to harden hearts and make a path for the deceitfulness of sin to destroy lives. Jesus, however, is the truth, and His death and resurrection leading to our freedom is absolute truth. His truths are woven throughout these pages for you to grab ahold of, by faith.

Friends, I see an awakening taking place in the body of Christ. An awakening to the true identity, transformation and freedom that comes with our salvation experience through our faith in Jesus Christ. An awakening to intimacy and a friendship with God that burns away the lies, unbelief and hardening of our hearts and also kills the desire for anything other than holiness – anything other than JESUS Himself. This book comes from that awakening in me. Although these pages contain many personal testimonies, prophetic words, dreams, visions and records of encounters with the Holy Spirit, you will find that they all point to Jesus and explain more about the true substance of our salvation, although not written in the format of a theology textbook.

This book is a *prophetic declaration* of John 8:36:

Whom the Son sets free is free indeed.

Free indeed. Not a *little bit* free. Not free only after many years of counseling (and believe me, I love and completely endorse counseling). Not free because maturity finally kicks in. Not free because I *finally* learned how to manage myself in my own strength. Free indeed, because that is what Jesus did, Who He is and who WE are in Him.

Ultimately, this is a book about JESUS.

Your journey through this book will take prayer. I ask that you commit to stay in scripture, anchor yourself to faith and ask the Holy Spirit to help you. God desires to reveal Himself to us in greater ways, so we must grab hold of His invitation in Jeremiah 29:13 and 33:3 to call to Him for His secrets and seek Him with our whole heart – not just with our minds.

I am so thrilled to do this journey with you! I am praying that as you read through these pages, scripture will open up to you like never before! I pray that the Holy Spirit would enlighten the eyes of your heart, and that revelation and understanding would abound. I pray that your love response to this revelation would overflow into the world around you. I pray that by the end of this reading, you will be shouting from the mountains, **"I AM FREE INDEED!"**

My hope is that you are encouraged to believe everything that He has done for us. Most of all, I am asking God to cause these words drive you deeper than ever into intimacy with your Jesus, to whom this whole book is dedicated.

Chapter 1
God on a Porch Swing

Before we start our journey, I want to establish one very important, foundational fact: *God's love is too good to be true.* We cannot understand it. We cannot explain it. We cannot change it. He is a truly good Father, and until this truth is lodged deep within us, we cannot fully believe that He has made us free and without lack. By faith in Jesus, a born-again Christian has been made *complete* (Colossians 2:10). We have the ability to come boldly before our Father to ask for help (Hebrews 4:16). The end of Romans 8 makes it clear that we cannot be separated from the love of God. And believe it when I say there is definitely no "catch" to this extraordinary love. It really *is* bigger than we can comprehend.

Before I go any further, I can hear some of your thoughts. *"I don't feel complete....what about my brokenness...if I'm supposed to be 'free,' why am I not seeing it in my life?"* All valid questions that I will answer in the following pages. Stick with me.

I have heard several ministers that I admire

say over the past few years that Christians need to stop fishing around in themselves, looking for what is wrong and what they can improve. Todd White, for example, says that believers need to just trust that they are new creations in Christ (2 Corinthians 5:17) and allow God to really "father" them. While contemplating this idea, the Holy Spirit showed me that sometimes, the chaos inside of me can be quickly brought to a place of peace by just being still, knowing that He is God (Psalm 46:10) and allowing His love to wash over me like a Father doting on His young ones.

Ephesians 2:6 says that I am seated with Christ in Heavenly places, which means that I am seated and resting in a place of authority and honor (Mark 16:19). I am seated – not striving to fix myself or fighting the chaos in my mind. I can *relax* in His Presence because I feel safe, secure and fully accepted.

Let me repeat that: I can *rest* because I know that I am *fully accepted* by my Father, thanks to what Jesus has done and my faith in Him. I can rest, and not constantly fish around to find something that needs fixing.

God on a Porch Swing Vision

One afternoon during a long nap, I dreamed that Father God was on a big, gorgeous porch like the ones I grew up sitting on in the deep South in the United States. The Father was swinging on a wide, wooden porch swing. Around the porch were children of God who had been at war or who had been contending and fighting to fix themselves, and they all stopped for a moment and put down their swords in order to sit in the swing with their Heavenly Daddy.

They chatted with God, they laughed with God, and they rested on His chest. I had a very strong feeling that God's preference for His children was to just sit with Him for a while rather than being in the constant chaos of warfare and striving. To sit as a child and let God be Himself; a big, strong Daddy that is safe and secure. I sensed that the children began to relax as they realized just how incredibly *loved*, valued and accepted they were. And as they looked to Him for approval, they grew stronger, wiser and began to look more like Him. *You see, they were starting to resemble what they were beholding.* They were carrying life and rest and child-like joy. They looked like their Dad, they talked like their Dad, they even had His mannerisms and His passion, and so they became aware of their true identity.

They were simply sons and daughters in His lap.

The Lord used this powerful dream to remind me that I can put down my sword and rest from the fight. I do not have to fix myself or clean up to just relax in His lap. Hebrews 4:16 says that we can come boldly to the throne of grace, and 1 John 4:16-17 says that since God's love abides in us, we can have confidence on the day of judgement because we are now like Jesus. You are like Jesus if, by faith, His love abides in you and you abide in His love. And the more you hang with Him, the more you realize you look like Him.

As for me, I shall behold your face in righteousness; when I awake, I shall be **satisfied with your likeness.** Psalm 17:15

Know His Tone

I used to be a dramatic arts teacher. Much of what I taught the students dealt with voice inflections, tone and articulation. An actor needs to learn how to properly use their voice to portray the correct emotions and present the audience with an understanding of how the character thinks and feels through the words they speak.

One of the activities that I used with my students was to have them repeat the phrase "*I said she didn't like him*" over and over, with a different vocal inflection on different words every time they repeated it. For example, if I said to you, "*I said SHE didn't like him,*" that would have a very different meaning from saying "*I said she didn't*

LIKE him." Likewise, if I put a firm emphasis on the word *"said"* and stated *"I SAID she didn't like him,"* you may think I was angry or annoyed when I verbalized it. The understanding of the meaning of the sentence all depended upon the tone and inflection from which the words were spoken.

This is a simple example of how people sometimes read the Bible and gain an understanding of God. If the reader "hears" the tone as harsh, annoyed or angry, they will see their Father in Heaven as such. This makes everything else hard to comprehend because the reader is wrongly interpreting what they hear. Many people do this when reading the Old Testament. They may read and hear a certain tone that appropriately screams wrath or smite, so they then misinterpret parts of the New Testament to mean that God lives life constantly angry, always ready to smite Christians who stumble or those who are not perfect, missing the entire point of the both covenants.

Likewise, a person who has had bad experiences with their earthly father may hear the earthly father's tone when they read scripture that appears to be more corrective or heavy, and it comes across as abusive or something to fear, instead of a loving father who has our best interest at heart. Unfortunately for many people, this is actually the case. Let me stop here and say, if this is *you*, Father God wants you to know that He knows, He cares, and He wants to redeem your idea of family. Let Him be your father – He lives to redeem the definition of FATHER for you.

Then there are those who grew up like me, knowing that my Heavenly Father's love was large and unexplainable and that my actual salvation did not depend upon my performance but by my faith. I knew that I was loved, forgiven and on my way to Heaven yet every time I read scripture, what I would "hear" is that I simply was not good enough, that I was not whole and that I had to really work hard to attain maturity and freedom. This made me feel an ongoing sense of unworthiness and exhaustion because I was also working hard to build a better ME.

As I mentioned before, I could not comprehend the thought of giving my entire self to Jesus because I thought I could not attain to what He was asking. Picking up my cross to follow Him brought fear and shame, yet my mind knew that it was by faith and not works that I had my salvation, and I knew that I deeply loved Him. I wanted to be holy, but did not see myself as such. The cycles of trying hard and failing were constant and confusing. I struggled at times to see myself as good enough to be a disciple of Christ, though I knew that He loved me regardless. My spirit knew one thing, but I was being taught another, and thus I lived insecure and divided. I would then read scripture through the tone of "not good enough," and so I constantly felt a sting of disapproval based on my own perceptions and confusion.

I fear that this is the same lie the enemy uses with many young believers, and the reason that some struggle to stand and remain "on fire." When identity is attacked and young disciples are not taught the truth about the beautiful *consequences of the tremendous sacrifice of Jesus,* the true substance of salvation, then they can find themselves on shaky ground and hugely distracted by self and trying to prove their holiness. Being self-consumed, even for what appears to be a noble cause, seems like a great tactic to keep someone from truly sharing in the overwhelming love and grace of God as well as being able to count the cost of discipleship. This skews the way people see God and also themselves, and soon they are wrestling in their own strength to prove something, instead of carrying the cross of Jesus as a love-struck son or daughter.

In my case, I often felt the voice of the accuser tell me that I would *never* be who God wanted me to be and that I would never, ever be able to prove myself. I also felt that I could never rest because I thought that I was always in need of constant maintenance. I was hearing and misinterpreting God all wrong because I was actually in my head more than His presence, and so I lived consumed by self and not by Jesus. I needed to hear HIS voice and tone.

When the voice we read with is saturated with the loving voice of a Father who is utterly enthralled by every fiber of our being, an awakening takes place within. Even if we cannot grasp the tone of His voice because it is far more beautiful than anything we have ever heard before, we must not run from it – especially when we think we do not deserve it. His love really IS too good to be true. And Father God is moved by even just a glance from our eyes!

For you reach into my heart. With one flash of your eyes I am undone by your love, my beloved, my equal, my bride. You leave me breathless—I am overcome by merely a glance from your worshiping eyes, for you have stolen my heart. I am held hostage by your love and by the graces of righteousness shining upon you. Song of Songs 4:9, TPT[1]

God actually adores us so much that I believe He lights up when we are in His presence. Setting everything else down to sit in His lap is not just for our own benefit. I am convinced that it is also for Him. *You minister to HIS heart when you worship*

Him, sit with Him and confide in Him. He loves us and delights in us so very much! If we do not know or believe fully this truth we will be in a constant battle in our minds, always trying to fix ourselves and living weary lives. We *must* establish the goodness of our Father and His unending love for us. We have to know that we are His friends and that He longs to sit on the porch swing with us. We are worth it to Him.

   "Out of all the humans, one person living with his heart in unity with Him was enough for God to keep risking everything. Just one person! From the one would then come the family. From the family would then come the generations. To God, we are worth the risk."[2]

It All Points to Jesus

When we read scripture or books like this or even hear songs or sermons that may make us feel slightly uncomfortable, we must remember to take it before the Lord and test what we are hearing. First of all, is the real Jesus being magnified? Is the Father's heart of grace, love and transformation being presented? Is there a healthy fear of God (reverence, awe, respect, trembling) and fire in the words, or is what you are reading/hearing bringing condemnation and shame *only*? If the way you read the Bible never points to the goodness of a God who is passionately pursuing relationship with you (over harsh punishment, shame and guilt), then you may need to go back to Him and ask Him to reveal where you are believing lies about Him.

Hebrews 12:6 says that He will discipline us like a son, so I am not talking about everything being fluff and sugary, either. But even then, a good father has the best interest of his children at heart, so we know that even in the discipline God passionately loves us and wants to see us aligned back to His heartbeat. Likewise, we know that the truth of God will never lead us to sin. He despises sin, but loves His children and gave His own Son's life so that we could be transformed out of a sinful nature.

The testimony of Jesus is one of redemption, transformation, reconciliation, restoration, resurrection power (yes, even in suffering), life and solution. His testimony is not one of fear, shame, guilt, or condemnation, or even of condoning sin. John 3:17 says that the Father did not send Jesus, His Son, into the world to condemn the world but to **save it**.

Let me make something clear: Jesus is love, but He is not mild, tolerant or tame. If you are stumbling over whether Jesus is the lion or the lamb, let me clear that up for you right now: HE IS BOTH. And He is wild and constant. When there is a healthy fear of the Lord on this revelation, and the fact that you have free access to this magnificent Jesus, nothing else will matter.

I want to reiterate the truth in Ephesians 2:6, that you are seated with Christ in heavenly places, and Ephesians 1:20, 21 which says that Christ was seated at the right hand of the Father, far above all rule and authority and power and dominion, and above every name. What this means is that God loves you so much that He seated you with His son, in His highest place of honor and authority. YOU HAVE SPECIAL ACCESS TO THE FATHER. He has given you this access simply because of JESUS in you, and not because you have been digging around in yourself trying to gain some unattainable level of maturity or self-awareness. Simply because He loves you, God longs to sit with you, to share His secrets with you (Jeremiah 33:3) and to give you a greater taste of what your salvation truly looks like!

Be Holy as He Is Holy

Holiness is the result of accepting Jesus by faith, repenting of anything that grieves His heart, and then beholding His face....and continuing to *just behold Him*. As you will see later in this book, intimacy with God is both our goal as well as the reason He came to give us this new nature – because He simply wanted to *be with us*. The more we dig deeper into His word, prayer and worship, and the more we begin to encounter Him, the more we begin to see ourselves looking like Him! Do not be kept from intimacy with Him because you believe the lie that you are not clean enough or He is not pleased with you. 2 Corinthians 5:21 says that you have been made righteous in Christ, and in righteous you get to behold Him. Righteousness is not a destination; it is your identity.

Your identity is righteous because God could not bear eternity without you. Jesus took the punishment, sin, pain, sickness and shame to make you acceptable, clean, holy and pure enough to be with Him forever. Jesus went through what He did to have intimacy with You. Yes, YOU. And not only did He provide a way into direct intimacy with the Father, but He also completely *changed your nature.* Your new nature is what gives you access to His heartbeat.

As I mentioned before, even if you are feeling the discipline of the Father at the moment, you can rejoice that you are being disciplined because you are a CHILD of GOD. Even if you are working through some difficult heart things, you can rest assured knowing that you are deeply loved, you have a new nature in Christ, and as your heart and thoughts align to His, you will begin to see how truly free you are.

Free Indeed

Just as the cover of this book states, once you learn to hear the heartbeat of the Father who is wildly passionate about your freedom, you WILL awaken to your true identity and the real substance of your salvation. You will begin to see yourself as **free indeed**, and you will see that you are no longer the old man, but a new creation in Christ. You will identify with being a son or daughter and a friend of God more than anything else, and it will be a more glorious place of abundance than you could have ever asked, imagined or expected.

His destiny for you will impact eternity. And you do not have to wait until eternity to begin to see it, believe it and walk in it. You are free NOW, if you choose to believe it.

Chapter 2
Oh Jesus, What Have You Done?

For years I felt like a fraud. A miserable fraud that was terrified of being seen as fake. Or worse... terrified of being truly SEEN, especially as someone who would never be mature and good enough.

Born-again.....most definitely.

Spirit-filled.....yes, of course.

Called to ministry.....working as a minister, actually.

But free.....not feeling it in the slightest. In fact, the idea of complete freedom confused and angered me because I never felt that I actually could attain to it, *even though the Bible said that it was mine.* What I felt about myself became the way that I interpreted the truth about my identity. I swallowed a lie, and this lie was holding me hostage to how I felt about myself. It caused unbelief in my heart, and thus made me more susceptible to ongoing patterns of sin, which I HATED.

I remember asking myself the unthinkable: *"What is the point of my salvation if I can't even get free here on earth? Why would You just get me to Heaven and allow me to live here as an emotional, broken mess, Lord? This is torture, and I'd rather just **die** and be with You than have to live this way until forever..."*

Dark thoughts started to come against me, and I engaged the lies that everything would be so much easier if I was just in Heaven with Jesus. Being here on earth seemed exhausting, and I felt I had the task of trying to fix myself on the inside so that I could perform better on the outside. I did not want to **own** my brokenness and depression like some ministers and Christian counselors taught. What I truly wanted was to be free from it, *absolutely and completely free.* And me taking my own life seemed a viable way of getting the peace that I desired, especially as I began to feel a self-imposed distance between myself and Jesus that I did not think I could recover from.

One day early on in my journey of understanding my new nature in Christ, in a moment of desperation, I cried out to God yet again. I had heard from a mentor in my life that I prophetically needed to hold God to His word, so I set out to do just that. It may be blasphemous to some, but I demanded that God do His job in my life! I asked Him to keep His promises, to give me freedom from this internal battle and to heal the hurt that resided on the inside of me. I prophesied from my heart that I WOULD be free, in the Name of Jesus. I declared myself healthy and whole. And of course, I sobbed and yelled, and then I soon fell into a deep, supernatural sleep.

In my sleep state Jesus came to me in a dream. In the dream I was sitting in a pit of mud. I sat with legs crossed, covered in yuck and weeping in complete desperation. After a moment I looked up, and Jesus was actually *sitting with me* in the mud. He, too, was covered in nastiness, and yet He still reached out to hold me while I cried. We sat together for a few minutes while His hug healed the ache in my heart, and then He stood up and offered to help me up. I realized quickly that I couldn't just stay in the mud. I truly had no desire to sit there in my misery, so up I stood with Jesus. The scene then changed to a very clean Jesus pouring both water and oil over a very, very dirty me. I felt the cool water roll down my skin and wash away the mud, while the warmth of the oil seemed to linger on my brow. Jesus then explained to me something that absolutely wrecked my understanding of what He had done for me both here in this dream as well as on the cross. Jesus said that He was washing the mud OFF of me, with great importance on the fact that He was not washing the mud OUT of me.

Jesus showed me that the misery, the brokenness, the sin and darkness were no longer inside of my DNA. *Darkness was no longer inside of my nature.* The sin and bad thoughts, though very real, were external to me. They were lies that I had partnered with which caused me grief and I certainly had to be cleaned off, but they were not part of me or my identity. And Jesus completely cleaned it all away.

When I woke up, I was laying sideways in my bed and found that I had a bit of sweet-smelling oil on my forehead! I had been home alone for hours and saw from the time on the clock that I had only been asleep for one minute exactly.

I was utterly in awe of the supernatural encounter I had just had. In fact, it haunted me for months after and brought up yet more questions for the Lord to answer. Being at the beginning of this adventure, I had no idea that He was taking me on a several-year journey of understanding of my identity and the *real* substance of my salvation.

My Christian world, up until this point, had been built on the belief that I was a sinner, saved by grace, and that I would always be just a little ole sinner that would forever struggle. I believed the lie that God's grace was big enough to save me from hell, but somehow not strong enough to keep me from sinful desires and torment in my mind and emotions. Everything in my walk until this point revolved around me trying my hardest to push away the misery, hide the brokenness and sin, and do everything I could to keep people from knowing the darkness that I *thought* was coming from deep inside my being and my nature. Not once did it even occur to me that all of this junk was external, coming from the enemy of my soul who only wants to kill, steal and destroy (John 10:10), and NOT coming from within my own new nature.

Now let me stop here and touch on something that many people could possibly stumble over. Although I definitely believe that not every thought or feeling we have is our own and is external, I do believe that there are regions of trauma and rejection that some people need to identify and be released from with the help of counseling, inner healing or deliverance ministry. Jesus can 1,0000% free us from these things in an instant, but sometimes when there are years and layers of trauma, lies, defense mechanisms, etc., at work in a person's life, they may need a little help. This does not, however, negate the truth that Jesus has given us a new nature, a new identity and has called us free indeed by faith in Himself (John 8:36).

This encounter ruined everything I thought I knew about what was going on inside the real me. What a journey I found myself on. Jesus was definitely about to show off.

Trust the Journey

I am sure that most readers can identify with my desire to be truly free. If you are anything like me after I first started asking God to reveal truth about my freedom in Christ, I was both skeptical as well as fully intrigued. Just as a prayer for salvation takes faith, so does a journey that goes against the grain of what we may have learned as young believers. I had to, by faith, **choose to believe** that if the Son sets someone free, they are truly free indeed. It is there in the Word of God, plain as day, and it is within context.

For me it took time, but my desperation to walk in freedom fueled the journey, as did my ongoing desire to go deeper into my intimacy with Jesus. Jesus Himself says that abiding in His word makes us His disciples, and that the Truth is what sets us free (John 8:31-32). The Truth found in scripture has the ability to set us free if we grasp it by faith, and it is our time with Him, processing this truth, that helps us to believe it as true.

Apart from the more well-known sins, there have been times where I have struggled particularly hard with things like depression, anxiety and fear, and also horrible thoughts of comparison. These may not sound like 'sin' to you, but anything that does not magnify truth and faith is not of God. There have been seasons where I felt like there was a brokenness on the inside of me screaming to get out and I was constantly shoving it down deeper and deeper just to get by. Having gone through years of counseling and finding some freedom in my thought life and my behavior patterns, I felt as if even my "right thinking" did not seem to be setting me utterly free from my sinful struggles. I finally believed the truth of Romans 8:1, that there is now no condemnation for me in Christ and that I no longer had to perform for God's approval, which brought a huge amount of relief and the ability to relax more in His presence. Yet I still felt so unworthy and broken, as if my tainted insides were about to seep through my very pores and destroy me as well as destroying my marriage and my ministry.

I always had chatter in my mind, the voice of the accuser telling me over and over that something was wrong with me and that I was a huge disappointment to people. In fact, *"what's wrong with me"* was a phrase that my husband banned me from ever saying! I would read books upon books about taking my thoughts captive and the mind being a battlefield. Although the content of my reading seemed to help a little, it never really solved the deeper problem. It was an endless cycle of digging up every sin that I could think of, and then, of course, repenting for it, and then reading Psalm 51 and Romans 8 over and over (and over). It was a good battle plan, and repentance is always a good thing, yet a month or so later I would be right back at the same place, even when the repentance was genuine. **Every. Single. Time.** I would always find myself right back at feeling broken and ashamed. Feeling a huge sense of lack and feeling like I would never be good enough while on the earth.

But God had me on a journey. He desires us to know that we are truly free indeed, and if you are seeking Him with your whole heart, He promises that you will find Him (Jeremiah 29:13). You will find Him, even if He has to chase you down with supernatural encounters like He did for me! He will never, ever give up on us. The journey with Him is imperative. Our friendship *with Him* is imperative.

Complete in Christ – Another Encounter

One night, I had a dream where I found myself in a top-down, convertible car with an Angel. The Angel was driving me up and down a beautiful, beach road. We could smell the ocean and feel the sunshine on our faces. This was the kind of road where one would want to rent a vacation home and stay for a few weeks of relaxation. However, there was so much construction along the road that we sensed a level of chaos and stress.

As I looked closer, I began to see that the homes on the road were being renovated. Each of them was on the beach but the sound of construction drowned out the beautiful ocean. There were homes of all sizes and shapes and colors, and yet every single one had some sort of work being done to it. I felt a little confused as to why the Angel was showing me this, and just as I was about to ask him why, he went a bit further and I saw that there was a big, beautifully constructed and fully complete home right on the beach. The Angel could see my mind turning, trying to work out what I was seeing, so he began to explain.

The finished house on the beach, he said, was **me**. Complete, beautiful and in a quiet and restful place. I kept looking back at the homes being renovated, and the Angel helped me to see that I was always seeing myself as just one, ongoing renovation. The sound of construction was always in my ears and thus choking out peace and the voice of my Father. I could never rest, and I never had peace in just being still because I always felt that I had to find something new to fix inside of my life, as if I would never be whole. He then reminded me that Colossians 2:10 says that we are "...**complete** *in Him, who is the head of all principality and power*" (NASB). I looked over at the completed home, and found it hard to believe how quiet and blissful it was.

Could that truly be a picture of ME, the REAL ME, in Christ? I had read Colossians about a dozen times and always seemed to miss that part. I remember waking up after this crazy dream and whispering aloud, *"Jesus, my Jesus... what have you done?"*

The idea that we are complete in Christ was another very important pillar in my journey to understanding what true freedom looks like. When a person lives in a place of always thinking that they are "a work in progress," they will never live like a free person. They will never truly speak like a person who carries authority and who moves in power. "*Signs and wonders follow those who believe*" (Mark 16:17), but what good is a belief in signs and wonders if you never feel that you are good enough or complete enough to perform them? Our destiny hinges on our friendship with God and thus knowing our identity, which is why the devil works overtime to keep us too distracted for intimacy and therefore blinded to our true identity. I could not even have a true friendship with God because of the unworthiness that I always secretly carried.

Even in my counseling and inner healing sessions, the shame of actually being there at all held me back from seeing the reality that these sessions were only helping to dismantle the structures I had built in partnership with the enemy. They were not another sign or more proof of brokenness. These kinds of healing sessions tear down scaffolding around an already beautifully clean structure, they are not the thing that makes you clean or whole. Only Jesus can do that.

We are destroying arguments and all arrogance raised against the knowledge of God, and we are taking every thought captive to the obedience of Christ –
2 Corinthians 10:5

And when you realize just how clean you are, because of what Jesus did, you will never be the same.

"Come now, and let us reason together, saith the Lord: though your sins be as scarlet, they shall be as white as snow; though they be red like crimson, they shall be as wool." – Isaiah 1:18

The Great Cognitive Dissonance

One of the biggest lies that the enemy throws at the Church is that she will never be able to be like

Him or walk in freedom or wholeness until we get to Heaven. I could not fully grasp the truth that I was free because I believed I could not walk in it. I knew in my heart that God's Word was clear and that nothing I did could separate me from His love (Romans 8:38-39), but striving became a bit of an addiction, and I always felt like I had a thousand, delicately spinning plates to keep in the air. Even having a finely written list of "who you are in Christ" scriptures was a struggle for me because I had no clue how to unpack some of the truths in these verses. What on earth did it mean to be "*dead to sin and alive to God in Christ*" (Romans 6:11)? And if I truly was dead to sin then why did I always feel so terrible if I tripped up? And what about the scripture that talked about being a new creation (2 Corinthians 5:17) or the fact that I am crucified with Christ and it is no longer me that lives but Christ in me (Galatians 2:20)? These passages bothered me so greatly that I often skipped over them when reading my Bible!

Most of my life, very few people could explain to me what these scriptures actually meant, and I was too fearful and stuck in lies to ask God to reveal them to me Himself. Thus, I clung to the verses that I could somewhat understand and identify with and decided to just live with the cognitive dissonance. But the problem I had was that I never seemed to be truly *free* from the thoughts and feelings. I was still tormented by my inadequacies and insecurities, though I knew I had power and destiny inside of me. The self-condemnation and self-loathing were something I learned to live with because I believed that all of my struggles were coming from within the very broken person that I was, and that I must therefore somehow deserve the torment. I even had strategies, accountability and specific fight plans in place to help me navigate life so that I did not feel quite so fake, especially being in ministry.

Yet I could not escape the heavenly dreams that I had, and the idea that perhaps I was already complete in Christ, because of my acceptance by faith in what Jesus did for me. And what about the dream of Jesus washing the dirt *off me*? He was emphatic that this nastiness was not *inside* of me, and He even allowed a supernatural occurrence of oil residue on my forehead just to push the point. But what did this mean? Jesus, what did you really do on the cross? I know that none of this could have happened in my own strength, and it certainly was not my imagination.

The questions still lingered. If Jesus died on the cross and rose again to save me, then did He only save me from hell? And if so, why do I still have to live in torment here on Earth? Again, if this is truly the case, then how am I *supposed* to be "holy as He is holy" (1 Peter 1:16)? If God is love (1 John 4:8), then why would a loving God *leave me in my sinful state*? Nothing made sense to me.

The dreams mentioned above, along with my friend Mark Greenwood's book, "*Awake to Righteousness*,"[1] drew upon the desperation in me to find answers to these questions, so I set out on an adventure to find out for myself what Jesus truly did on the cross. If all His death and resurrection did was pay for my ticket to heaven and make me acceptable in God's presence, then why would God drop bombs in scripture like Romans 6, which states that we are free from sin, or even John 8:36, "*Whom the Son sets free is free indeed?*" And why did I still feel so yucky in His presence, as if I could never push any deeper than where I had already been with Him?

I felt a strong invitation from the Lord, and I knew that I was hearing the tone of a loving Father, so I knew that there must be more.

And I was SO right.

Time to Hope Again

Can I give you some hope? I have briefly shared some of my past struggles with you, but I want you to know that today I KNOW that I am completely transformed on the inside. I am free indeed because Jesus made it that way, and by faith I have accepted this as truth. I will explain more later about our new nature in Christ, but please hear me when I say that being free indeed is not just a lovely goal to work towards or a great title for a book. I am free indeed because I have grabbed a hold of the fact that I am a child of God and I have accepted the truth that I have been utterly transformed in my nature. I have worked with the Holy Spirit to rip down any lies or scaffolding that has tried to set itself up against the knowledge of what Christ has done for me (2 Corinthians 10:5), and I have begun to rebuild my life upon the truth that Jesus died so that I could be free.

"As He is, so am I...." – 1 John 4:17

I now see that Jesus' radical act of passionate love was one that I may never fully understand, but it is everything that makes me who I now am. I am not just slightly free, but ***utterly transformed*** because of Jesus. Do not believe the devil's lies that you will never be free. Whom the Son sets free is absolutely free indeed (that is you, if you are born-again). You are free. Even if your emotions, your heart and your thoughts are catching up with this truth, it does not make it null and void. Even if your heart is throbbing with pain from torment or trauma, please accept these words as hope for your healing journey. Maybe the journey is not in "getting free," but in KNOWING that Jesus has already made you free, and now you get to walk out that truth with Him as you rip down the external structures that have held you in torment.

There is so much in my Spirit that I want to share with you. I want to encourage you to continue pushing in deeply for more revelation from the Holy Spirit during this journey. Keep going to the Father for answers, and continue to stay connected to His heart. There is SO MUCH that He wants to share with you as His friend, apart from this book. He is our everything.

Chapter 3
Jesus Within

I hope that by now, you are starting to ask more questions. I pray that even if there is a tension in your heart, that you are drawn to Jesus in these words. His words are beautiful, and His heart is FOR YOU. That is why freedom is so attacked – because you were created for fellowship with Him, and bondage keeps you out of pure fellowship.

We **demolish** arguments and every pretension that sets itself up against the knowledge of God, and we take captive every thought to make it obedient to Christ (2 Corinthians 10:5). I hope that you will allow me to continue to demolish all pretenses that have set themselves up against the knowledge of what Jesus has truly done!

As I have already mentioned, though I am now aware of my freedom and my new nature in Christ, I have lived most of my life with feelings of self-condemnation and guilt. It has been one heck of a journey to believe the truth and see self-loathing broken to pieces. I only share my journey with you to show you just how faithful God has been, and just how free and transformed on the inside that Jesus has made *you* as well. I want to give you tools to demolish anything that sets itself up against the knowledge of God, and what He (Jesus) has done.

Before I believed that I had a new nature in Christ, one of the things that I struggled with was lying. Sometimes just "little white lies" as the world would call it, and other times massive whoppers came forth from my mouth if I felt afraid. Sometimes it looked like a slight change of narrative to save face, other times it was merely deflection or misdirection. Many may see nothing wrong with some of these, but I want to remind you that scripture is clear that anything that does not promote truth is a lie. *"The LORD detests lying lips, but he delights in those who tell the truth"* (Proverbs 12:33). So, every time I would default to lies to guard myself or protect myself from the torment of potential rejection, I would spiral into dark thoughts again and withhold my affection from Jesus out of shame. Although not a pathological liar, I would say things in a panic if I thought I had to smooth something over when I had let someone down (which I always felt I was doing). I absolutely hated it. It made me feel dark and ugly on the inside because I was giving in to my fears. And I absolutely hated the guilt and shame that it brought with it.

I was confused by this behavior in myself because on one hand, I knew that I was born-again and had the Holy Spirit inside me, but on the other hand I felt so enslaved to the fear of man and the fruits of that fear (lies being one of them). As I shared before, I would repent, read through Romans chapter 8 and remind myself that there was no longer any condemnation for me because I am in Christ Jesus, and then I would feel "free" for a few weeks until it came back – sometimes, returning with a vengeance.

The Grace Revolution

There was an awakening in the early 2000's, that many agree, was the beginning of the Church at large feeling a sense of frustration over these same issues. I absolutely honor those who took a stand in the face of religious spirits and preached the message of God's grace and our undeserved favor in Him. The messages about how toxic and harmful condemnation can be actually set an entire generation on course for finding the truth about what actually happened on the cross. Although the enemy entered pockets of Christianity and twisted the truth of the gospel to wrongly glorify sin, there were others of us who stood for the truth, in spite of the hyper-grace excesses, with the passion and fire of Paul the Apostle when he said in Romans

6:1-2, "*What shall we say then? Are we to continue in sin that grace may abound? By no means! How can we who died to sin still live in it?*" God's grace is not **not, not, NOT** an excuse to sin, but something that empowers us not to do so. Grace alone, however, does not solve the problem of sin itself. How sad that so many missed this.

During this grace revelation movement, many old religious mindsets were broken off me and others who had come from religious backgrounds. One of the main things that pierced my heart was that I had been made free from guilt and shame. In the past, when I would give into fear and act according to my old nature, I would struggle for days with feeling physically ill or depressed, which were products of the condemnation in my life. When I realized that this is not who I am and not how God sees me, I felt a sense of freedom and a lightness that I had never experienced before. It was a glorious feeling as I went deeper and deeper into a greater understanding of who I am in Christ. My intimacy with Jesus subsequently grew deeper for a time, and this was foundational for where I am today.

Breaking the religious mindsets off the Church were incredibly necessary for a season. **But freedom from guilt does not equal freedom from sin.** Although I knew how to combat some of the feelings of guilt and shame because of my revelation of grace, I still struggled with what I thought was a darkness coming from *within* the real me, as if it was hard-wired into my being and would forever keep me in a state of being "unholy" or "not good enough." I still longed for true freedom.

It Won't Come Off

God is so good to me. He always speaks my language! Dreams happen to be one of the biggest ways that He shows me things, apart from my reading of scripture. I love it when He articulates His heart to me in prophetic dreams, especially when I know that it is a dream to be shared with other sons and daughters. I live to *"equip the saints for the work of the ministry..."* (Ephesians 4:12).

This particular dream is one that I refer to often to disarm any old lies that the enemy tries to throw at me. In this dream, I had stepped in something smelly that had stained the bottom of my foot. I tried everything that I could to remove the stain and stench: Vinegar, turpentine, oils, soaps, scrubs, etc. Nothing would remove that nastiness! I tried covering it up with nice shoes, but people still kept getting faint whiffs of the smell. It was super embarrassing! I even tried making it pretty by painting my toe nails and getting nicer sandals and even tanning myself to try and even out the colors. All to no avail.

After some time had passed in the dream, I was exhausted from not being able to hide the smell or change the appearance of this stain. I felt so at fault, like I was a failure as a Christian for not knowing how to remove the stain on my foot. I felt like my worst fear had come to pass: That finally, all the darkness inside of me had seeped out and that this darkness *was* the stain on my foot, and not just something that I had stepped in. In my desperation I yelled out to God to please fix this so that I could actually start to live a normal life! And in His awesome goodness, God reached down in the dream and picked me up. The next moment I saw myself standing in a gorgeous, babbling brook in a meadow where Jesus stood before me. As I began to weep in His presence, He leaned down and washed my foot in the brook, and it finally completely removed the stain and stench. He held me for a second, reminding me of His love and His complete lack of judgment for my inability to clean my own feet, then He smiled at me with such love, affection and enjoyment – and I woke up.

The reason I believe so strongly that this dream is one for the body of Christ is because it completely exposes several lies of the enemy. The most obvious lie is that we sometimes feel like we have to try and cover up and hide the sin in our lives, and that if we do no one will know it exists. I hate to bust any bubbles out there, but sin will *always* be exposed: "Everything that is hidden will be shown, and everything that is secret will be made known" (Luke 12:2).

Another lie is that God holds judgment against us for our inability to keep ourselves "clean." This is a lie that has kept people in bondage for ages, and part of the reason the "Grace Revolution" helped so many. The third lie of the enemy is that we can handle it on our own, striving in our own efforts to get clean while not needing to share our struggles. James makes it clear that we are to confess our sins, pray for one another and find healing (James 5:16). We don't have to carry things on our own! And the fourth and probably the most sinister lie of all – *that we have darkness, rather than Jesus, inside of us that will start to seep out of us unless we do something quick to hold it back.*

The Truth About the Darkness Within

This is the message we have heard from him and proclaim to you, that God is light, and in Him is no darkness at all. – 1 John 1:5

I have been crucified with Christ. It is no longer I who live, but Christ who lives in me. And the life I now live in the flesh I live by faith in the Son of God, who loved me and gave himself for me. – Galatians 2:20

Every good thing given and every perfect gift is from above, coming down from the Father of lights, with whom there is no variation or shifting shadow – James 1:17 (NASB)

If you are born-again, you have actually been crucified with Christ (see Galatians 2:20). Being crucified means that you have DIED. You were crucified WITH Jesus, so all of your fleshly desires, your sinful nature, your shame, your sickness and mental health – all of it died when He died. And guess what? When He rose again into newness of life, He was still without sin...and so are you. And if you keep reading Galatians 2:20, you will see that you are actually *so dead* that it is now Christ living inside of you, along with the Holy Spirit. It is as if you have come into existence all over again. This is what Jesus meant in John 3 when he talked about being born-again.

Regardless of how you were born, you have been born-AGAIN into His DNA, His nature, His Kingdom of light. Reborn. Renewed. Regenerated.

We will talk more about all of this in the next chapter. But for now, if you do not believe me, have a look also at 2 Corinthians 5:17-21.

Therefore, if anyone is in Christ, he is a new creation. The old has passed away; behold, the new has come. All this is from God, who through Christ reconciled us to Himself and gave us the ministry of reconciliation; that is, in Christ God was reconciling the world to Himself, not counting their trespasses against them, and entrusting to us the message of reconciliation. Therefore, we are ambassadors for Christ, God making His appeal through us. We implore you on behalf of Christ, be reconciled to God. For our sake He made Him to be sin who knew no sin, so that in Him we might become the righteousness of God.

We are new creations. We are reconciled to God. We are restored to our original design. He makes an appeal through us, calling us His ambassadors. Can you believe that we are now His righteousness?! Now there is some hope right there! Let's also look at Romans.

You, however, are not in the flesh but in the Spirit, if in fact the Spirit of God dwells in you. Anyone who does not have the Spirit of Christ does not belong to Him. But if Christ is in you, although the body is dead because of sin, the Spirit is life because of righteousness. If the Spirit of Him who raised Jesus from the dead dwells in you, He who raised Christ Jesus from the dead will also give life to your mortal bodies through His Spirit who dwells in you. – Romans 8:9-11

Going back to 1 John 1:5 and James 1:17, John states that there is no darkness in God. And if there is no darkness in God, not even a shadow – and God now lives in you – is not the logical conclusion that there is NO DARKNESS in YOU??? Remember, there is no sin nature inside of one who has been born-again. There may be strongholds and what I call "scaffolding" to rip down, but this is not hiding inside your nature or in your new make-up.

Important side note: The word darkness in 1 John 1:5 is the Greek word *skotia* which means lack of light, but also means wickedness and things done in private that result in misery.[1]

The thoughts that we think that do not produce or increase the Light but bring misery – such as the phrase, *"what's wrong with me"* – are not coming from within us. This is an external thought planted by the enemy to keep us in bondage and self-consumed. This is why intimacy with the Father and renewing our minds in His truth are so important. We must not partner with the lies that try to keep us in torment, and we need the Lord to speak His love, acceptance and realigning truth over us directly and continuously. The reason that my husband banned this particular statement from being said in our home is because he could see that every time I repeated it, I was partnering with a demonic voice whispering in my ear. And with every agreement and partnership, another stronghold is built and set up against the knowledge of God!

Also, to be clear and avoid any confusion, when I refer to "darkness" I am speaking of sin, wickedness and a sinful nature. I am not referring to demonic possession or traumas that need help dismantling.

The Truth About You

For at one time you were darkness, but now you are light in the Lord. Walk as children of light. – Ephesians 5:8

I have learned that the truth about me is that I am not a liar, I am not an insecure person and I do not reek of brokenness. Jesus has changed that. I am full of truth because the Spirit of truth lives within me. I have nothing to prove and nothing to hide because I know who I am. I know that I am not the kind of person who lives in fear of man, thus producing fruits of sin. I produce the fruit of the Holy Spirit (Galatians 5) because I am a new creation in Christ, completely transformed by Jesus and what He did for me. PERIOD. And I know without a shadow of doubt that there is zero darkness within me and nothing wrong with me because I am dead to it and He dwells within me. And I can daily remind myself of these truths when I look at my Father, face-to-face, and allow Him to wash His love over me again. If I happen to give in to the fear of man, I am either believing a lie and need to repent and replace it with truth, OR seek help in ripping apart the strongholds in my mind that are keeping me in bondage to this lying fear. Either way, the truth about me remains that I have been transformed by Jesus, and He is alive and at work inside of me.

If you are struggling to grasp this truth for yourself, let me ask you this question: ***Who told you that something was "wrong" with you?*** It certainly was not the Holy Spirit. The Bible says that there is no condemnation for those in Christ Jesus (so His tone would *not* be condemning). The Bible in Romans 2:4 says that it is the kindness of the Holy Spirit that leads to repentance ("something's wrong with you" definitely is not a very kind thing to say). The Bible also says in John 16:8 that the Holy Spirit comes to convict the world of sin but He convicts His believers of *righteousness*. We were convicted of sin when we first got saved, and now He exposes any lies that we may be believing that would cause us to act contrary to our righteous nature. He is a good Father and may need to redirect our steps, realign our thinking and expose lies we may believe. He may discipline us in love, but He will never accuse or fault find. That job is already taken by the devil (Revelation 12:10).

I am convinced that thoughts like "what's wrong with me" or "I'll never be good enough" come from external, demonic sources. The devil is a liar, and the father of lies and there is no truth in him (John 8:44). The devil is rejected, without hope, without peace and incredibly ticked off and thus will do whatever he can to taint the thinking of a born-again child and contaminate your mind and behavior to be like his.

You may need to let that sink in for a second.

Precious friend, there is nothing WRONG with you. There is only something that needs realigning in your thinking if you believe that you are just a little ole' sinner saved by grace that harbors darkness within. *You are no longer a dirty sinner.* You have been crucified with Christ and it is now Him that lives in you. Read Romans 6 if you do not believe me. We MUST stop labeling ourselves in direct contradiction to what the Bible says we are! And for those of you who may be wondering about Romans 7, my amazing husband will touch on that in a coming chapter.

I speak over you now as we dive into deeper revelation waters that you have the mind of Christ (1 Corinthians 2:16) and the helmet of salvation to guard your mind (Ephesians 6:17) and you have weapons of warfare that are NOT of this world (2 Corinthians 10:4). This is an invitation to USE the weapons the Lord has given you. You are on a beautiful journey to complete freedom and the enemy will do whatever he can to keep you blind to the truth. You ARE the RIGHTEOUSNESS of God in Christ Jesus (2 Corinthians 5:21).

In the next chapter we will look at some of the scripture that the Lord used to grab my attention and reveal to me the truth about what He really did. I will share my thought processes and how the Lord drew me to the conclusions I came to regarding my new nature in Christ. Together, we will explore why the "good news" is indeed truly GOOD NEWS!

Stick with me friend. Freedom is YOURS, in Jesus Name!

Side Note: The Question of Demons in Christians

The question comes up often regarding can Christians have demons. Most of my life, I was taught that this could not be possible because of the Holy Spirit living within a believer. I tend to agree that a born-again Christian can NOT be *possessed* by a demon. However, I do believe, even despite the idea that Jesus died to make us free indeed, that Christians can indeed have demonic influences in their lives, and often in their bodies.

I believe that this is often a matter of semantics – possession, oppression, demonization, to name a few terms that cause confusion – and sadly, many in the Church have done a poor job of teaching and stewarding this topic. But I have seen enough in my 20+ years of ministry, as well as in my personal life, to not agree that demons can indeed influence and torment Christians, even spirit-filled ones.

If a Christian opens the door to the demonic – for example, through things like lying, drugs, porn, adultery, fantasizing, being fascinated with darkness, etc. – this is called a breach. If the breach stays opened, ie. The Christian remains unrepentant and/or leaves the breach opened, this gives the enemy legal ground to have his way in the body, emotions, mind and life of a believer. This in no way means that a demon can get into a Christian's spirit, or fully possess their body, but spirits have access to torment those who have not chosen to repent and close open doors to the devil, or who refuse to forgive. Sometimes demonic influence comes through deeper wounds such as trauma or abuse. Either way, it does not change the plans of God for that Christian, or his new, regenerated nature.

Here is a deeply personal example. There was a time, as a pastor who passionately loves Jesus, when

I was consistently partnering with a spirit of death, and consistently allowing the external thoughts that *"life would be better if I were gone"* to consume me. I even had a plan to take my own life, if things grew to be too hard. This kept a heavy demonic oppression on me and I was living in a cycle of depression, until one day my husband commanded this foul spirit to get OFF of me, in the mighty Name of Jesus. I will never forget that moment, as began to scream almost uncontrollably while I literally felt something heavy and unseen come off my head! In a moment I was delivered, and after seeking help from a counselor and repenting, closing doors, and completely saturating myself in the word and truth of who Jesus made me, I never felt that foul spirit return. I firmly believe that I was delivered from a demon that day.

Although I cannot present a full theological debate on the subject of Christians having demons, I do believe that understanding our new nature in Christ is imperative. And, with the help of the Holy Spirit, beginning to dismantle the lies of the enemy with the truth that whom the Son sets free is free indeed, we can begin to walk in the authority that Jesus promised we would have. The Holy Spirit is wonderful at dismantling lies, ripping down that scaffolding we build around ourselves, and revealing truth. If we lean into Him, get help where needed and seek after truth with everything we are, we will experience lasting freedom.

Let me return our thoughts to Jesus, before I close out this chapter. Our precious Jesus, the One who died and rose again so that we could be free. The man who, Colossians 2:10-15 states: *"and in Him you have been made complete, and He is the head over every ruler and authority; and in Him you were also circumcised with a circumcision performed without hands, in the removal of the body of the flesh by the circumcision of Christ, having been buried with Him in baptism, in which you were also raised with Him through faith in the working of God, who raised Him from the dead. And when you were dead in your wrongdoings and the uncircumcision of your flesh, He made you alive together with Him, having forgiven us all our wrongdoings, having canceled the certificate of debt consisting of decrees against us, which was hostile to us; and He has taken it out of the way, having nailed it to the cross. When He had disarmed the rulers and authorities, He made a public display of them, having triumphed over them through Him."*

Our wonderful Jesus, who did all this so that we could be forever with Him.

Take a moment to thank Him for all He has done.

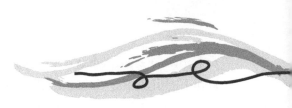

Chapter 4
The Virus is Dead

A huge revelation for me has been in knowing that living a transformed life is not a process of doing a list of things to act transformed, but believing that we already ARE transformed. Therefore, what if finding ourselves free indeed is not a journey toward identity, but simply just *believing* that this *is* our new identity in Christ, and then beginning to tear down the old scaffolding and build our lives upon this truth? How differently would you live if you knew that you could walk in complete freedom?

What does it mean to be *crucified with Christ* and *dead to sin* (Galatians 2:20 and Romans 6:11)? What if you knew that this is actually your inheritance and the true substance of your salvation? As a friend of mine said to my husband once after receiving this revelation, "*No wonder it's called the GOOD NEWS!*"

God was so gracious to take me on an adventure in finding truth. My husband seemed to have a better grasp of some of this than me, but I wanted to know *for myself* what it all meant. For years God kept highlighting Galatians 2:20, Romans 6:11 and 1 John 4:17 to me over and over again. Anyone who is involved in the prophetic knows that when something repeatedly appears in your sights, God is most definitely trying to speak through it! I read up on these verses, and I read as much as I could from other writers who had different perspectives. Some of them obviously heard God's voice in a very different tone from me, so I took any gold from them that I could and began to ask the Holy Spirit to show me what I was missing.

And then one day I began having the dreams and visions mentioned in this book. God was speaking to me, and He was speaking loudly. Much of what my friend Mark said in his book "*Awake to Righteousness*"[1] made sense to me, but I still wanted the revelation for **myself**. And God graciously began to give it to me in these dreams!

Please allow me to guide you through my thought process as I came to the conclusions that I am absolutely free indeed. Please note that this is not a theology text, a doctrinal debate or even just a glimpse from my journal. This is the Spirit-led thought process I had in coming to believe this truth. Also, this is not the exhaustive list of the scriptures that God showed me; I am only sharing the scriptures that were real rhema words to me on the journey. If you dig deeper, you will find that God has so much more to say about freedom in His Word! I firmly believe that this chapter is going to bring great freedom and insight. I am SO excited for you.

I do invite you to pray the Ephesians 1:17-18 prayer over yourself, asking God to give you a spirit of wisdom and revelation and enlighten the eyes of your heart in the knowledge of Him so that you can know the hope to which you have been called, and the glorious inheritance that you have as a saint. Find a quiet, intimate spot with Him and let Him pour His love over you. Remember, you can always ask Him questions and trust that He will respond (Jeremiah 33:3).

I just want to stop here and remind you – Jesus is SO GOOD. I hope that you are starting to see that He did so much more for us than we can think or comprehend. I am thrilled for Him to reveal Himself more and more to you, and to me, in the coming pages!

Thought Process 1: Crucified with Christ

*I have been **crucified with Christ**. It is no longer I who live, but **Christ** who lives in me. And the life I now live in the flesh I live by faith in the Son of God, who loved me and gave Himself for me.* – Galatians 2:20

I read this verse probably a hundred times in my life, and could never understand its meaning. How could I have been crucified *with* Him??? Past churches taught me that Jesus died *for* me, not that I died with Him. I understood that it is all by faith in the Son, and that He loved me and gave Himself for me, and now lives inside of me etc.... but the part that says "*It is no longer **I** who live....*" that bothered me greatly. I also saw that Romans chapter 6 speaks of us being "dead" as well, and yet no one knew quite how to explain it all to me. Therefore, I started asking the Holy Spirit to show me the true meaning of all this *dead* talk.

Here are some more scriptures that began to pop out at me on a regular basis. It was as if God was using a Spiritual highlighter that would catch my eye every time that I saw these verses:

*We know that our old self was **crucified with Him** in order that the **body of sin might be brought to nothing**, so that we would no longer be enslaved to sin.* - Romans 6:6

*For you have **died**, and your **life is hidden with Christ** in God.* – Colossians 3:3

*In Him also you were circumcised with a circumcision made without hands, by putting off the body of the flesh, by the circumcision of Christ, having **been buried*** *with Him in baptism, in which you were also raised with Him through faith in the powerful working of God, who raised Him from the dead.* – Colossians 2:11-12

*Therefore, if anyone is in Christ, he is a **new creation**. The old has passed away; behold, **the new has come**. -* 2 Corinthians 5:17

Remember the dream I mentioned a few chapters back, where I was covered in mud and Jesus poured water and oil over me and then told me that the mud was not *inside* of me, but *on* me? I began to think of this dream in relation to 2 Corinthians 5:17. My thoughts were this: If I am indeed a new creation **in Christ**, with an old self that has been crucified (brought to death), and if Jesus and a powerful Holy Spirit now lives in me, *then how on earth can sin reside inside me???* This was a hard one to grasp because of what I had always been told about sin, and about my **maturity being defined by how well I avoided sin.** Darkness represents sin to me, so to further make me see that sin was no longer in my nature, God also pointed me to a few verses regarding darkness.

*For at one time you were darkness, **but now you are light in the Lord**. Walk as children of light.* – Ephesians 5:8

...God is light. In Him there is no darkness at all. –
1 John 1:5

Through this, the Lord reminded me of when I was 7 years old and first prayed the sinner's prayer to ask Jesus into my heart. I attended a Christian school at the time. I was always a very creative child who loved the arts, bright colors and nature. One morning in chapel, the teacher showed a clip art photo of two hearts. One was a dark, black heart that had yucky stuff scribbled in it, and the other was a white heart that had rainbows coming out of it with the core of the rainbow heart itself being pure white. She explained that the black heart is our heart *before Jesus*, and the white heart with rainbows is what happens to our hearts *after we accept Jesus*. She then gave an invitation to pray the sinner's prayer.

Being the creative, color-loving 7-year-old that I was, *of course* I wanted my heart to be clean enough to have rainbows coming out of it! Who would want a yucky, black, scribbled in heart? I invited Jesus to come into my heart and make it pure and rainbowy. That was decades ago.

I believe the Lord reminded me of this event from years past because it is a beautiful example of what does happen in our hearts before and after salvation. The Lord does not just dye our hearts white, He GIVES US A NEW HEART

COMPLETELY. And that new heart is full of promise and life!

I established in the last chapter that there is no longer any darkness within us as born-again believers. No darkness = no sin in our nature. We still have the capacity to sin, but like my dream explained to me, it's no longer a part of our natural selves because we are born-AGAIN. We have actually died to sin and the power that it held over us. Let me explain with a very simple explanation that Holy Spirit shared with my husband and myself.

My husband and I used to be big Sci-Fi geeks. In many Sci-Fi programs that we have watched, there is a story-line where a character has some sort of dark, nasty thing enter their body. Imagine with me a dark spot in the heart of man; a kind of virus that begins to spread throughout and take over the host, much like sin for the pre-redeemed man. In these Sci-Fi programs people are usually influenced by the virus even though they try everything possible to be rid of the dark spot within. Often the only way of getting rid of it is actually killing off the character completely. The Holy Spirit showed my husband that the best way to kill a virus is to kill the host! I did some research on a number of medical and science websites, and the truth is that any virus *needs* a host to survive.

Without a host, there would be no virus. And how interesting to note, many of the larger viruses (like the black plague) actually ended up eventually *killing off their host.*

This makes me think of sin. It will eventually kill off its host. "For the wages of sin is death…" (Romans 6:23). But if the host can be killed off first, the virus would cease to exist.…

….no wonder we had to be *crucified with Christ!!!!* The virus had to die. WE had to die so that sin could be found dead and powerless in us. Romans 6:6-7 says it this way: ***We know that our old self was crucified with him in order that the body of sin might be brought to nothing, so that we would no longer be enslaved to sin. For one who has died has been set free from sin.***

I hope this is helping paint a picture for you like it did for me. We are dead to our old nature so that we can be free indeed from sin completely! We are not just covered by what Jesus did on the cross, we spiritually died *with Him* and rose again *with Him* into a new life. We have a new Spirit and a new nature, and it is completely free from that virus of sin.

Thought Process 2: Dead to Sin

So you also must consider yourselves dead to sin and alive to God in Christ Jesus. – Romans 6:11

My husband Carston, who is an amazing teacher and prophet, began to ask God for a way of explaining this scripture in simple, easy language that would be a powerful tool for teaching. If you know Carston, you know that he consistently pours over the scriptures and always seeks truth – sometimes at a great cost. I am so glad that he has allowed me to share this with you[2] because I believe it is a powerful illustration of what Jesus *truly* did to make us free indeed.

While asking God for insight, the Lord brought my husband into an open vision. In the vision he saw a scantily clad woman sitting on the side of a street that he was walking down. She had a sign around her neck that said "SIN." She had two bouncers with her, both had the word "TEMPTATION" written on their shirts, and both of them were trying to strong-arm Carston into going over to this woman.

In the vision, he tried everything he could think of to get away from these guys. He tried avoiding them and walking a different way, yet they chased him down. He tried taking a very large and muscley friend with him, yet they still came after him and overpowered them both. He even tried to wrestle them himself, to no avail. Finally, my husband remembered that he had a card in his pocket that said "*dead to sin.*" He pulled out the card and showed it to the bouncers, who then quickly backed off and did not bother him again. This "*dead to sin*" card held more power than anything else that my husband could have done in his own ability to be free from the temptation in front of him.

For some reading this book who have never had an issue with lust and sexual sins, please do not tune out! Pretend that the woman representing "sin" actually represents whatever it is that you, personally, have struggled with. The same applies to us all – in Christ, we are *dead to sin*. It is no longer on the inside of us, and we no longer have to rage against our flesh to keep it at bay. Sin is external and the only power it holds over a believer comes from what we *think* about it.

I feel like some of you may be asking the question that if sin truly is external – meaning it is no longer coming from within our newly redeemed and purified beings – and if the Bible says that we are dead to sin (remember, we were crucified with Christ and sin was killed with us on the cross), then *why do we still sin?* That was the very next thought in my own thought process, so I am happy to share it with you as well. I am sure some readers have been asking this question all along.

Thought Process 3: Adam and Eve
Believed a Lie

This revelation about believing lies seemed to really tie everything together for me. The first question I asked myself after getting the revelation that I was free indeed and dead to sin was this: "*Then why do I still sin?*" That is a valid question! God led me to the original sin, found in Genesis chapter 3:1-7.

Now the serpent was more crafty than any other beast of the field that the Lord God had made. He said to the woman, "Did God actually say, 'You shall not eat of any tree in the garden'?" And the woman said to the serpent, "We may eat of the fruit of the trees in the garden, but God said, 'You shall not eat of the fruit of the tree that is in the midst of the garden, neither shall you touch it, lest you die.'" But the serpent said to the woman, "You will not surely die. For God knows that when you eat of it your eyes will be opened, and you will be like God, knowing good and evil." So when the woman saw that the tree was good for food, and that it was a delight to the eyes, and that the tree was to be desired to make one wise, she took of its fruit and ate, and she also gave some to her husband who was with her, and he ate. Then the eyes of both were opened, and they knew that they were naked. And they sewed fig leaves together and made themselves loincloths.

What caught my attention was the serpent's response to Eve regarding the reasoning that God gave them for not eating the fruit. The serpent said to Eve, "*For God knows that when you eat of it your eyes will be opened, and **you will be like God**...*" Eve ate and shared with Adam, who also ate, because *they believed that they would be like God.*

But have a look at Genesis 1:27 regarding when Adam and Eve were first created: "*So **God created man in his own image**, in the image of God he created him; male and female he created them.*" As closely as Adam and Eve walked with God, surely, they would have known that they were actually made in His image. They would have been exposed minute-by-minute to the true tone of the Father's heart and voice, so they would have been aware of His love for them and that He had their best interest in mind when He asked them not to eat that particular fruit. But the devil, who the Bible says is crafty and has no truth in Him (Genesis 3:1 and John 8:44), lied to Eve about her identity. He lured her into believing that she could attain, by her own doing, an *identity* that was actually *already* who she was.

Eve believed a lie, and therefore gave the devil power. This opened the door to sin, and therefore stripped Eve (and Adam, once he ate) of their original design, which was that they looked like

God. The demonic is always subject to what we allow, so when we allow external voices to lie to us and define us, we are essentially trading our original design for a counterfeit.

God revealed to me through Adam and Eve, as well as my husband's bouncer vision, that we still have the capacity to sin, but we only give way to temptation when we believe lies that the devil feeds us. Hebrews calls sin "deceitful." Remember when I said that the only power sin holds over a believer comes from what we *believe* about sin? Eve ate and shared with Adam because she thought she would become someone beyond what she already was. I used to stretch the truth, and even fully lie, because I believed that I was a disappointment and that others would not approve of me if I was completely honest about my failings, flaws, desires, etc. Many people struggle with anxiety and depression because they are still believing the lies that there is something wrong with them, and they have allowed self-condemnation to define them instead of their righteous nature in Christ (2 Corinthians 5:21). Some people choose to sin simply because they have no idea that they are truly free indeed. Still others have a scaffolding of lies to protect them due to past traumas, and they need help in dismantling these things and experiencing the love of the Father as He gently shows them who He created them to be…His unique child, who walks with Him in freedom.

The good news is that we can confront the lies and disassociate ourselves from them through the power of truth and faith in that truth. Romans 6 says that the power of sin has been broken through our "death" in Him, which means we are no longer obligated to allow the demonic activity in our lives. With the Holy Spirit inside of us and our deep intimacy with the Father, the Holy Spirit and with Jesus, we have the ability to, by faith, partner with the truth of what Jesus has actually done.

I may sound repetitive, but we honestly *need* time abiding in the heart of our Father to remember that we have the Holy Spirit inside of us, and thus we have the ability to keep His commands. "*The one who keeps His commandments abides in Him, and He in him. We know by this that He abides in us, by the Spirit whom He has given us*" (1 John 3:24). We must "abide" in order to not fall into the traps that sin sets for us.

Sin is deceitful, plain and simple (Hebrews 3:13). We must stay in the Secret Place at all costs, and allow the love of the Father and the truth of who we are in Jesus to wash over our minds and hearts and renew them. Sin hardens the heart, and in the end brings us nothing but death and sabotage (Romans 6:23). But oh, Praise be to our wonderful Jesus, who has set us FREE from the power of sin and death (Romans 6:7-11)!

A Power That's Broken

I AM TRANSFORMED. The old Mandy is dead. I have been restored to the image of my Creator. It is no longer Mandy that lives, but Christ within me. And any thoughts, even the feelings or desires that are contrary to truth, are external lies that have no power. I can just pull out my "dead to sin" card and remind the enemy (and myself) that the power of sin is broken – is DEAD – in my life.

One last personal testimony to let Jesus speak for Himself.

For many years, from the time I was four years old, actually, I had a nervous habit of picking the skin off of my fingers. I would do it so regularly and so often that my fingers would stay raw. They were *always* bleeding or torn up, so in 30+ years, I never had my nails done because it was just not appropriate for a professional to have to deal with my disgusting fingers. Growing up, I tried everything in my own power to stop – I even tried putting hot sauce on the open wounds and wrapping them in bandages to keep myself from picking at them! Praise Jesus I have never had an infection from my stupid and futile attempts to quit. As a married adult, I would even hide my "picking" under a blanket or under the table so that my husband would not see. I was so ashamed.

A few years ago, as I was understanding this more and more, I said to the Lord that if I was truly free indeed, I wanted to be able to walk in complete freedom and be able to get my nails done professionally as a statement of the transformation that had taken place within me. God graciously exposed some lies I had been believing as well as the root lie that actually first caused this behavior all those years ago, and I was completely *set free* after about an hour of debunking lies and grabbing hold of truth. I called my husband sobbing the next day, because it had been the first and only day in about 35 years that I had not touched the skin on my fingers! I remembered that I was alive to God in Christ and dead to sin, and the power was broken. All praise to Jesus, Who now IS my identity. And gosh, do I love getting my nails done now!

Transformation – that is the real meaning of salvation! I pray that hope is arising in you now as you begin to see and understand that Jesus went through what He did not just to cover your sin, but to remove your sinful nature.

*...Behold, the Lamb of God, who **takes away the sin** of the world! – John 1:29*

Chapter 5
The Elephant in the Room

If you are like me, you are soaking up these truths, yet still have a few seemingly contradicting key passages of scripture in the back of your mind. Most of us would have grown up reading these verses out of context and therefore remained unknowingly in bondage to sin because we felt subconsciously justified by what we read. After prayer, reading these passages *in context* and study into the original Greek meaning, the Lord helped me to disarm any lies I was believing that kept me stumbling over the following three passages. I have also had the enormous privilege in the past few years of being surrounded by solid, mature pastors and leaders who have helped me to process these scriptures. I think it is always healthy to discuss Jesus-truths with other mature leaders.

Once again, this is not a theology book or an exhaustive list of scripture. I know that there may be other passages that you may have questions about, but for the sake of time and consistency with the tone of this book, I will only unpack the few that I wrestled with in the past few years. I do, however, provide in the back Appendix a list of further reading and teaching for your own study.

Also, I think it important to note, this is from my personal journey into the revelation of what my salvation truly looks like. My journey may be different from yours, and my way of thinking and processing may not look the same. I do not expect your questions or thought processes to look identical to mine, but I do believe that the Lord took me on this journey in order that others can glean at least a little of what I learned. If you still have questions, I implore you to seek out answers with the Holy Spirit, and allow Him to teach and lead you into all wisdom and revelation in the knowledge of Jesus Christ (Ephesians 1:17).

I am also thrilled to introduce you to my husband, Carston Woodhouse, as I have invited him in this chapter to expound upon the end of Romans 7. But first, here are a few of my own conclusions about other scripture.

Unpacking Truth in Context

1. **1 Timothy 1:15 (NKJV)[1] – "This is a faithful saying and worthy of all acceptance, that Christ Jesus came into the world to save sinners, of whom I am chief."**
    Yes, you have read that correctly – Paul

clearly refers to himself here as the "chief of sinners." This verse used to make me feel a sense of justification if I sinned, because if someone as amazing as Paul was the "chief" sinner, then surely it was ok if I stumbled a bit at times too. But as Paul says in Romans 6:1-4: *"What shall we say then? Are we to continue in sin that grace may abound? By no means! How can we who died to sin still live in it? Do you not know that all of us who have been baptized into Christ Jesus were baptized into His death? We were buried therefore with Him by baptism into death, in order that, just as Christ was raised from the dead by the glory of the Father, we too might walk in newness of life."*

Sin is never an option, and we are dead to it. So, what is Paul **really** saying in 1 Timothy?

If you look at the Greek word for chief, you will find that the word Paul uses here is *prōtos*,[2] which means *"first in rank; former."* What Paul is stating is that he was the first in rank of all-time sinners, not that he was *currently* a sinner at the time that he wrote to Timothy. In modern terms, it is as if Paul was saying that he had won a medal for the fastest 5km race in high school, and no one has beat his record since then. Paul is no longer a runner or in high school, but he still holds the fastest record. Or another example would be the highest score on the old Pac Man arcade games at the skating rink that I would visit as a pre-teen (I am showing my age now!). There was always that one kid whose three little initials we could never knock off the board, no matter how hard we tried. One summer we found out that the initials actually belonged to a kid who did not even live there anymore, it was just that no one could reach his high score. Paul is saying that if his sin was a Pac Man game, his initials would be at the top. *Thanks to a merciful God, Paul used to be the chief of sinners but that is no longer his current state as a born-again believer.* And it is no longer your state either, if you are born-again. If you read in context, Paul is actually talking just before this verse about false teachers who had snuck into the church to teach the law again, and he is making it clear that Jesus came to save sinners, something that the law could not do. Paul (who was once Saul) knew about the law and transformation of Jesus all-too-well!

2. **Jeremiah 17:9 – "The heart is deceitful above all things, and desperately sick; who can understand it?".** I only recently grappled with this one while writing this

book. I have been told most of my life to not trust my heart because it is wicked and deceitful. So then how do I justify saying that sin is external and the blackened heart is transformed if my heart is full of deceit? God pointed me to Ezekiel 36:25-26 to explain.

I will sprinkle clean water on you, and you shall be clean from all your uncleannesses, and from all your idols I will cleanse you. And I will give you a new heart, and a new spirit I will put within you. And I will remove the heart of stone from your flesh and give you a heart of flesh.

The Prophet Jeremiah was around before the prophetic priest Ezekiel, and Jeremiah had a different "tone" than Ezekiel. "*Jeremiah was called to proclaim many messages of reproof and solemn predictions of doom over his people for their disobedience*"[3] while Ezekiel is described as a prophet whose "*prophecies include some of the most soul-stirring word pictures of God's relationship with His people, the importance of each of its individuals to Him, and of the eternality of their mission.*"[4]

So yes, the heart of mankind *without Jesus* is deceitful. Remember, Jeremiah was prophesying on the other side of the cross. But as Ezekiel prophetically declared so boldly to a people who had yet to meet their Savior, a day would come when mankind would be given a new heart and a new Spirit. He even went a step further to say in verse 27: *"And I will put my Spirit within you, and cause you to walk in my statutes and be careful to obey my rules."* The icing on the cake for me is that Jeremiah actually alludes to this in 24:7 when he says, *"I will give them a heart to know Me, for I am the Lord; and they will be My people, and I will be their God, for they will return to Me with their whole heart."* This is most definitely a reason to rejoice!

Disclaimer: I do believe that if too much abuse or trauma affects a person, and they shut down or heavily guard their "heart" (mind, will and emotions) in an ungodly way, that this can make room for more lies, more demonic strongholds and yet higher scaffolding that needs to be ripped down. But as for the heart of a man – the seat of his conscience and moral character – the Lord says that He has removed the hard heart and given us a new, soft, Jesus-like version. A heart that John states, does not condemn us.

"By this we shall know that we are of the truth and reassure our heart before him; for whenever our heart condemns us, God is greater than our heart, and he knows everything. Beloved, if our heart does not condemn us, we have confidence before God." – 1 John 3:19-21

I am honestly still working out the language for all this, and again the word "heart" is often used by many different groups to mean different things, so I do not want to bring confusion over semantics. Yet I can say with confidence, my head and my Spirit know the truth: There is no deceitfulness or sin *inside of me* anymore. I have a new heart, and a new spirit, and I am a completely new creation in Christ. Colossians 1:27 says it this way: "…*Christ IN you, the hope of glory.*" My identity in Christ is completely new – all of me.

Remember my rainbow heart? My heart is full of Jesus and thus full of promise and life. I sometimes stand in awe of how amazing this truth is. It is in time abiding with Him, as His beloved, that I see this truth clearly and learn to see myself as the new creation that I am.

And now…I am so excited to introduce you to my amazing husband, Carston Woodhouse. You will find that Carston's writing style is very different to mine, and yet we so perfectly compliment one another in the way that we teach and unpack truth. I know that his words will give you great clarity, and you will find so much freedom when you grasp the revelation that the Lord has given him!

Romans 7 – Carston Woodhouse

I feel like this chapter, especially verse 15 of Romans 7, onwards, has lived in the back of my mind. Perhaps it has lived in your mind, too, like an unconscious justification for sin that we can fall back onto if we or someone close to us ultimately gets stuck. A way of explaining if some great leader, or a hero of the faith, makes a mistake – much like the falsely soothing explanation for all sin. But unfortunately, this same crutch, like holding on the edge of the pool, has kept us from freedom. If we are willing to let go and truly understand the meaning of these verses, we may just lose our "excuse" for sin – our safety blanket – but we will also get to swim in the wide waters of His actual forgiveness, the wonder and beauty of true Godly sorrow, and walk in freedom from sin.

Likewise, we may be using the Law as our pool rail, because "*without it, wouldn't we just go on sinning wilfully?*" So, we stay in self effort, rather than allowing Christ to live through us by His Spirit. However, like a child hanging from a tree branch, if we are willing to let go of the Law – our own efforts to live Holy – and just live by the Spirit, The Father will catch us. Or, better yet, we may realise that by

The Spirit, we no longer have an inherent desire for sin, and we can fly.

To understand this, we must take a look at WHO and WHAT this chapter is talking about. Context is important.

Begin to ask the Holy Spirit now for the grace and wisdom to understand and receive from the Word.

Paul is NOT Talking About a Christian

Verse 5 makes it perfectly clear that referring to a Christian is not what Paul is about to do. It states *"For while we were in the flesh, the sinful passions, which were aroused by the Law, were at work in the members of our body to bear fruit for death. (NASB)." Stay with me: "But now we have been released from the Law, having died to that by which we were bound, so that we serve in newness of the Spirit and not in oldness of the letter."*

You see, Paul writes Romans 7 not to justify the sin of a Christian, but to demonstrate that the Law could not lead to Holy Living. Paul wants to point out that we needed a better way to serve God: The Spirit.

This is THE WHOLE POINT of this chapter, and as you will see, there are a couple of questions the Apostle Paul has to navigate in order to explain this.

Why Paul Even Goes There

It would be completely understandable to ask at

this point, "well, if it's not talking about a Christian, why even go there?" Great question. Allow me to break it down.

3. **The law cannot make you Holy, we need a better way.**
Paul has to demonstrate and explain the inadequacy of the Law to make us Holy in practice. God has now given us a better way to serve Him in Holiness: The Spirit. If you actually understand the problem, then what the solution has achieved will make way more sense.

4. **Is the law then bad?**
Paul has to explain how this can be true, and yet how the Law can still be Holy and good. They all knew, as we do, that the Law is from God (especially the Jewish believers of the day). They knew that God definitely spoke to Moses. So, while the Law cannot save us or make us Holy, it is definitely Holy and from God. This begs to ask, if the Law is not the true problem, *then what is?*

5. **How can we be free of the Law?**
We must know that the Law holds everyone accountable unto death. Thus, how can we be free of its jurisdiction (its authority to convict and condemn)?
I have listed these questions in a logical order

that our minds, being familiar with the scriptures already, would ask. However, because of the order in which Romans 7 is written, we are going to answer them in the reverse order.

So, firstly, question number 3.

"How can we be free of the law?"
Right from verse 1, Paul states his case. "*The law has jurisdiction over a person as long as he lives.*" When we are baptised into Christ, we share in Christ's death. When He died, we died with Him. (Rom 6:1-7, Gal 2:20, 2 Cor 5:17). Now that we have died, we are released from the law, like a marriage where one spouse has passed away, and are then free to be joined, or "married" to another. We are now joined to Jesus, and are one spirit with Him.

So, this takes us to question 2.

"SO…does this mean the Law is bad?"
Great question, and Paul answers it in verses 7-9. In fact, Paul asks it in an even more intense way. He asks, "*is the law sin?*". HUH? How can the Law be sin?

Let us go back a couple of verses to explain. Verse 5 says "*For while we WERE in the flesh, the sinful passion, which were **aroused** by the Law, were at work in the members of our body to bear fruit for death.*"

What does all that mean? He is saying that, before we came to Christ, we were in this situation called "the flesh". In this state, we had controlling desires for sinful things inside of us, and the Law stirred them up. Imagine you had this nasty little alien living inside of you, and whenever you saw the right thing to do (God's Law), it made you want to do the opposite. Instead of loving, it made you selfish. Instead of purity, it made you lust. So, when you say something like what Paul was saying, you could almost think it was God's Law that was MAKING you sin. You will notice when I quoted verse 5, the word ***aroused*** is bold. This is because in the original Greek language (in which Paul wrote this letter), that word aroused is not there! It was put there by translators to help the verse make sense. If we take it out, it sounds like Paul is saying the sinful passions were BY The LAW. Go back and read it again, but this time read it without the word aroused. IT SOUNDS LIKE PAUL IS SAYING THE LAW PRODUCED SIN. And, ironically, Paul intended it to sound like this. We know this because the very next thing you would think was, "…***wait, are you saying God's Holy Law is bad, or even Sin itself?***" He wants you to ask this question, because the answer is VERY important, and it is contained in verses 7-12. I am going to summarise these verses: ***Is the Law sin? (or what made us sin?). No. It was not the Law that made us sin, but this thing called sin that was living inside us. The Law made me know what sin*** *was, but this thing called sin that was inside took one look at God's Holy Law and made me do the opposite, and this produced death.*

Ok, but does that mean that this holy Law – that should bring life – actually produced death? No again. It was this thing called sin that was inside me that produced death. It is SO BAD, that it used God's Holy Law to kill me by making me sin. You see the Law, because it IS Holy and Pure, righteously demands my death.

This whole situation seems like sin has taken advantage of God and His Law, and now has the upper hand. But not so. Now sin has been revealed, like diagnosing a deadly parasite. **The Law itself was not the problem – this thing called sin is.**

Now that you know what it is, and that it is in there, you know you need to do something about it. You need a saviour to get you out of this situation.

So, lastly, Question 1.

As we saw above, Good and Holy as it is, The Law can't make us Holy (because of sin on the inside), so what is God's solution?
Paul actually really answers this question very early in the chapter, Verse 6 states, "*But now we have been released from the Law, having died to that by which we were bound, so that we serve God*

in newness of the Spirit and not in oldness of the letter"

In case you are wondering, "oldness of the letter" means the Law. It was no good having a perfect instruction manual to life and holiness if we had something on the inside causing us to do the opposite. Except that the Law, like turning the light on in a room full of cockroaches, revealed the sinfulness that was in us. But now we have been provided a better way to deal with the situation. Instead of trying to live up to a set of Laws that were on the outside, but having sin on the inside, now *in Christ*, He has put His Spirit inside of us. This Spirit, Who, instead of producing the desires of sin, gives us new desires and produces a life of Holiness.

By the way, that is why God can take us new creations out from under the Law, because we do not need to be kept 'under the Law' to prevent us from sinning. If you take a person who has not yet been born again out from under the Law, you give them a license to sin, because that is what they desire to do. But we no longer need to be kept under the law to stop us from sinning, because **by The Spirit** we no longer have the desires of our old sinful nature, but a desire for Holiness.

But what about those classic verses that "everyone" points to if a Christian sins? Now, let us take a look at the classic verses from Romans 7, verses 15-22.

"For what I am doing, I do not understand; for I am not practicing what I would like to do, but I am doing the very thing I hate. 16 But if I do the very thing I do not want to do, I agree with the Law, confessing that the Law is good. 17 So now, no longer am I the one doing it, but sin which dwells in me. 18 For I know that nothing good dwells in me, that is, in my flesh; for the willing is present in me, but the doing of the good is not. 19 For the good that I want, I do not do, but I practice the very evil that I do not want. 20 But if I am doing the very thing I do not want, I am no longer the one doing it, but sin which dwells in me. 21 I find then the [n] principle that evil is present in me, the one who wants to do good. 22 For I joyfully concur with the law of God [o]in the inner man, 23 but I see a different law in [p]the members of my body, waging war against the law of my mind and making me a prisoner [q]of the law of sin which is in my members. 24 Wretched man that I am! Who will set me free from [r]the body of this death?"

A conflict of two natures? I don't think so!
Many translations have this heading in the middle of Chapter 7. By stating that this is a "conflict of two natures," it is somehow suggested that a war going on between two relatively equal

natures; or at least that both sides have the capacity to win, even if just occasionally. Even worse, as I once believed, that the passage is describing a war between the flesh and the Spirit. Not only are both these interpretations in error, they are not even what the verses literally say. Now look at them in order and in context:

1. A war that can be won or lost?

As we read through these verses, we do not see Paul EVER winning. This is not an arm wrestle; in fact, it is TOTAL DEFEAT. He cannot win. Not by the exertion of his own efforts or devotion, nor even his spiritual maturity. More accurately, here he is a *complete slave*. Having to do things against your will, and being unable to do what you will to do (that is, to HAVE to forcibly obey someone or something else's will) is the very definition of slavery. To even suggest that a Christian is ALWAYS forcibly enslaved to ALWAYS SIN is not only absurd, but a complete contradiction of Romans chapter 6, which describes us as having been set free from sins' slavery.

But to our point, what Paul is doing is describing a battle that can never be won, neither by any effort nor will power, not some difficult battle that we could slowly get better at, and perhaps sometimes win. What we need is not some self-improvement/spiritual growth process, we need A WAY OUT OF THIS WHOLE SITUATION, and that is exactly the point. AND, exactly what the Gospel provides. It is one of the reasons why the blood of Jesus is better than the blood of the Old Testament sacrifices. Instead of having this impossible situation of trying to obey the Law, but failing, we now have a better way, a new way. We have died to the law, and now live by The Spirit.

Verse 5: "*But now we have been released from the Law, having died to that by which we were bound, so that we serve in newness of the Spirit and not in oldness of the letter.*"

Now we have a way of Holiness that works, and we have been released from the contract to the Law that did not work because of the sin that previously ruled us.

I also want to note, the Law is binding on a person until death. To be released from the Law, you have to die. This is what happens in baptism (see Romans 6:1-7), our old sinful self dies, and a new creation arises with Christ. This is also why Paul starts chapter 7 by explaining the whole '*if a woman's husband dies, she is free from the law concerning her husband and can marry someone else*'. Now we can be freed from the law (which did not work because of the sin we had within us), and be joined to Christ, no longer to try and live by an external law, but by the Holy Spirit who now lives in us and produces Holiness from within.

So that begs another question. Is Paul describing a battle between the old force of sin (or if you like: the flesh) vs the new Spirit within us?

2. **The bondage he describes is not between the forces of flesh and Spirit, but between his mind and sin.**
Verses 15-24 NEVER mention the Spirit. What 2 force does he say are involved? 1) His Mind, and 2) Sin.

The struggle is between his *mind*, and the *force* (or law) *of sin* that was within him, not The Spirit and Sin/or flesh. And sin ALWAYS WON.

In his mind he had decided he wanted to obey the Law, but there was something in him (sin) that prevented it. Even worse, this thing called sin in him took exception to God's Law and made him do the opposite, try as he might. This is exactly the slavery that the Law of the Spirit sets us free from, as we will see in Romans chapter 8:1-4.

Galatians 5:24 says that those who are of Christ HAVE crucified the flesh with its passions and desires. Thus Paul, who also wrote Galatians, is not here describing a war between his flesh and Spirit, but between his mind and the sin in the flesh (which we see in Romans 6 died with Christ).

This leads us to a couple more questions about that big chunk of verses we read earlier about doing the thing he doesn't want to do, and so on… verses 15-24.

Why Does Paul Speak in Present Tense?

One of the biggest confusions around these verses is the fact that they are written in the English present tense. From this we could assume, as many have argued, that Paul must be talking about his present condition and experience. Not so. It is entirely possible to tell a story using present tense language, even though it clearly happened in the past. Allow me to demonstrate by telling a story about an event that happened while I was body surfing some years ago:

"So, I'm looking at this 6-foot wave coming, and I'm like, let's do it. I start booking it, and suddenly I'm on this thing, on my stomach, and I'm starting to surf down the front of this 6-footer. I'm going so fast, and it spits me out like a cannon, and I just start skipping across the water like a stone on my chest. And every head there turns and looks, and it's, "WOAH!""

As we can see, I have definitely used present tense language much of the time, but it is very clear to you all that I am talking about something that happened in the past. By going back into the moment, I bring you personally into my experience, so you can relate to it internally, because those who were familiar with the Law could relate to Paul's experience of trying to live Holy. By demonstrating his own experience, and bring those familiar with the Law into it, he is also able to demonstrate the solution, and demonstrate how it differs from, and is far better than what they have known under the Law.

Verse 25 – Why That Word Order?

"Thanks be to God through Jesus Christ our Lord! So then, on the one hand I myself with my mind am serving the law of God, but on the other, with my flesh the law of sin."

At first, the verse sounds like victory, but then he says he is serving the law of sin. Then the chapter ends!?

I spent weeks reading this verse over and over with Holy Spirit. Then it hit me: THERE'S NO CHAPTER BREAK IN THE ORIGINAL LETTER, ONLY IN MY BIBLE. Paul is just summarising the situation he just described, probably because it was such a lot to take in. The very next sentences completes the thought – the first verses of chapter 8. Let us put it all together without the chapter break, and I am going to add a little note to help us:

"So then (to summarise all that we have been talking about), on the one hand I myself with my mind am serving the law of God, but on the other, with my flesh **the law of sin.** *Therefore there is now no condemnation for those who are in Christ Jesus. For (Because)the law of the Spirit of Life in Christ Jesus* **has set you free from the law of sin and death."**

He makes it clear. In Christ Jesus, this slavery to the 'law of sin and death' that he just described in such detail, you have been set free from by the 'law of the Spirit of Life'. **That is it**. In Christ you have been set free from this whole situation cycle of sin and death. **That is why** there is no condemnation for you in Christ. You are not doomed to a life of sin that flows to death and judgment.

An important note in all this: Grace does not justify peoples' actions (sin); it only justifies people.

Having the correct understanding that Romans 7 is NOT demonstrating a struggle of a Christian, but the impossibility of living Holy by The Law, in the flesh, means we can rightly understand Romans 8, particularly verses 1 and 3.

When we read verse 8:1, *"**There is therefore now no condemnation for those is Christ**"*, assuming that Paul just described a Christian, we can interpret it, as I once did, that there is no condemnation simply because we cannot help but sin. But this is not true, and robs Jesus' blood of its credit, and its reward. Grace is not God 'winking' at sin because He thinks we cannot help it. Grace is ACTUAL FORGIVENESS, where we did the wrong thing and Jesus paid a terrible price to completely forgive us, and set us free. Now we see that there is no condemnation in Christ because the blood of Jesus has paid for and cleansed us. We are no longer under the Law, so there is no longer any jurisdiction for it to condemn us. And death is no longer at work in us to produce this horrible lifestyle of sin. Now we have a new river flowing from within us. Now we have a better way to serve God – the new way – THE SPIRIT.

Unlike the Law, which, while Holy and Perfect, could never make us live Holy because of sin which lived in us; The Spirit produces perfect holiness in oneness with Jesus. Which, by the way, is also perfect fellowship, WE CAN FREELY APPROACH HIM BECAUSE HE HAS MADE US ACTUALLY HOLY ON THE INSIDE, something the Law could not achieve, which is why there was a veil between them and God that needed to be torn. It is, in no uncertain terms a prophetic picture of the inability of the Law to bring us into His Presence. (See Hebrews 9:8)

The finishing point, Roman 8:2-5

"For the law of the Spirit of life in Christ Jesus has set you free from the law of sin and of death. 3 For what the Law could not do, weak as it was through the flesh, God did: sending His own Son in the likeness of sinful flesh and as an offering for sin, He condemned sin in the flesh, 4 so that the requirement of the Law might be fulfilled in us, who do not walk according to the flesh but according to the Spirit."

Now, thanks to Christ Jesus, the horrific cycle of bondage to sin and condemnation while we were **in the flesh** and **under the law**, has been broken by The Spirit.

As we saw, verse 2 states that the law of the Spirit of Life in Christ Jesus has set you free from the law of sin and death – the very thing Paul describes being in bondage to in chapter 7 in those classic verses above.

In Summary

That's a lot. I know.

So, let's put it in a nut shell.

The Law cannot make us Holy. The problem was not the Law, but this thing called sin inside of us. It *made us* sin, even if we wanted to follow God's Law. And that sin meant death. So, instead, Jesus made a way for us to get out of this situation. How? First, we died with Him, so we could be freed from the Law and from sin. Next, we were raised to life with Him by the Holy Spirit, Who now lives in us. Last, He lives in and through us to produce the Holy Life and perfect union with Him that God always desired for His people. Paul sums it up best in Romans chapter 8:2.

This is such an important time in history as He restores a revelation of the fullness of what the Gospel REALLY DOES. He does not just forgive our sins; He cleanses us from sin. He sets us free. *This is especially important in this generation in light of different doctrines and questions about Grace that the enemy is pushing that excuse continuing in, or even permitting various sins.*

You are FREE INDEED if you are born again. And Paul proves it all in Romans.

God Does Not Justify Sin –
(Back to Mandy Woodhouse)

While praying into this chapter and discussing Romans 7 with Carston, I asked God for a greater wisdom (for myself) on how to share this revelation. My entire life I had leaders use Paul's words here to justify the fact that they were struggling, and this seemed to be the passage that people would turn to over and over to "help" me when I actually asked about how to get true freedom from sin. I know that many of the body of Christ probably have the same association with Romans 7, and I have prayed for an awakening to take place so that people no longer feel in bondage to sin as I did for so many years. One day in the shower, after having wrestled with Him over this chapter, I heard Him say clear as day, "***Mandy, as if I would EVER want to validate your sin.***" Wow, what a revelation!

If you're still struggling with this passage, I do encourage you to read Romans 5-8 over and over again, asking Holy Spirit to reveal truth as you meditate on the words written. Let God's word speak for itself. He will never validate sin, so why would we think this is what Paul, of all people, would be talking about? Everything before and after Romans 7 sets up Paul's argument that JESUS is the only One that sets one free from sin.

He *sets free from sin*. He never validates it.

I told you it was all about Jesus!

The Adventure Awaits

I feel strongly like this is an invitation for YOU to enter into a grand adventure with Him! Proverbs 25:2 says, "*It is the glory of God to conceal things, but the glory of kings is to search things out.*" We are kings and priests under the New Covenant, and I believe it is to our glory to search out the hidden things of God. "*Call to me and I will answer you, and will tell you great and hidden things that you have not known*" (Jeremiah 33:3).

The whole of the Old and New Covenants point to Jesus and what He has done to transform our nature, but I am not unaware that there may be other verses that you may "trip over" in the process of finding out for yourself what God wants to say to you about this. If there are blocks of scripture that you have questions about, I want to remind you that when you read the New Testament from the New Covenant perspective, keep in mind that Jesus IS the context. If something does not line up with what Jesus has done, who He is or the fact that we have been made new in Christ, then perhaps the context of what you are reading needs to be reevaluated. There is no need to feel fear or to gloss over scripture that does not make sense, just ask Him for revelation. That is what I did in the above scriptures, and I am confident that the journey of faith in finding the answers I needed has changed my life in more way than just simply understanding a context.

As I type this paragraph, I am sitting at a lookout spot in sunny Brisbane, Australia, where I live at the time of the first publication of this book. Carston is from Brisbane and I have visited here a number of times before moving here from the USA in 2019. Over the years I have heard about all the best cafes and restaurants and tourist attractions – but living here is more than knowing all about it. In my adventure of actually residing here, I have explored, gotten lost more times that I would care to admit, and I have come to really know my way around. My experience with Brisbane has grown into an intimate, knowing experience because of my many personal adventures and explorations. I am the type of person who had to get lost in the city to finally know my way around. I believe that this latter illustration is a good one to describe the journey of intimately knowing these revelations for yourself. Get lost in the Word, explore the New Covenant, search for Jesus in the Old Testament, be a friend of God and allow Jesus to meet you with the intimate knowledge you hunger for.

No More Excuses

When I finally, by faith, accepted the truth that I am completely free from that deceitful sin and free from my flesh, everything changed for me. I was, for a lack of a better word, **ruined** for any other belief. I began to read scripture differently as it actually came alive to me, and even my intimacy with the Father and with others deepened. And how I now see Jesus – I am in awe of Him like never before! I also stopped focusing on the things I thought I lacked, and started to see myself as I actually am. I have no excuses left to still act like a sinner.

The time has come for the Bride of Christ to stop believing the lies of the enemy about what her identity *is not*, and to accept God's invitation into the identity that Jesus paid for. We are free indeed because the Son set us free. We died *with* Christ, and rose again as one who no longer lives but has Christ within. We have an entirely transformed nature that allows us to walk free from sin's grasp and free from things like anxiety, depression and fear as well, should we choose. God's gift of grace forgives us and covers our sin and allows us to come into His presence, but His gift of righteousness makes us free from sin completely. As His sons and daughters, as His friends, we have full access to Him and to all of His promises. It is time we start to *believe* it.

The Bible says that the anxious longing of the creation waits eagerly for the revealing of the sons of God. (Romans 8:19, NASB). That is you and I. Creation is waiting for us to see that we are sons and daughters with righteous natures. It is time for truth to be revealed to us so that we can shine!

Those who are wise shall shine
Like the brightness of the firmament,
And those who turn many to righteousness
Like the stars forever and ever. – Daniel 12:3

Chapter 6
You Are NOT a Person with an Issue

By now you probably see that I am pretty passionate about Christians understanding the true substance of their salvation, and walking out the supernatural identity that Jesus paid for us to have. For far too long the enemy has wreaked havoc within the life of the Church, causing many voices to be stifled or silenced by fear or lack of understanding. Too many people have fallen prey to the tactics of the enemy, giving way to sinful lifestyles because they have no idea that the "reality" they are living in is counterfeit, and they have therefore pulled away from intimacy with Jesus because of the lies they have partnered with. Likewise, many God dreams have been aborted – all because His children had no idea they are actually free indeed.

Intimacy is key to continuing to walk in the freedom that Jesus paid for. He tells us in John 8 that it is truth that sets us free, and that truth is found in the Word of God. Likewise, we abide in Him in order to not sin, and this is clearly seen in 1 John 3:24, "***Whoever keeps his commandments abides in God, and God in him.** And by this we know that he abides in us, by the Spirit whom he has given us.*"

One of the most profound revelations regarding my intimacy with God on this journey has been knowing that I am His daughter. This part of my identity was pivotal in growing my understanding that I am free from shame, free from striving, and free from sin's power. Being able to come and climb into His lap, fully accepted and with all the security in the world revolutionized the way that I approached my time with God. For far too long I had seen myself as someone with "issues," and thus became distracted from God's plans, my dreams and supernaturally deep intimacy with Him because I was trying to sort those issues out. When I realized that I was a daughter and I was safe in my Heavenly Dad's presence, issues or not, I found myself walking more intimately with Him than ever. In His presence, as a daughter, is where this book was birthed. And in His presence is where I learned that I am no longer a woman with "issues."

A Vision of the Feet of Jesus

At the end of 2018, I was living in Aiken, South Carolina, USA, but spent some time in Brisbane,

Australia – one of my favorite places on the planet. I am married to an Aussie so I have been fortunate enough to go back and forth across the two countries for years now, and at the time of this book's first publication I would have only recently moved back. It is actually a prophetic word over our lives (as a couple) that we are a bridge between the two nations, ushering people and prophetic words from one land to the other, and we have certainly been that! In October of 2018 I was attending an Australian Prophetic Summit. As I was enjoying the prophetic event and already in an environment saturated with His presence, you may well imagine how greatly prophetic and vivid my dreams were that week! But I had one recurring dream that absolutely rocked me and exposed one of the major lies I was believing regarding my identity.

It started a few nights before the first session at the Summit. I dreamed about the feet of Jesus. In the dream His feet were massive, and I felt so small in comparison. I tried to pull myself up slightly, but I felt in myself that I just could not, so I stayed down at His feet. I woke up slightly and thought to myself, that was one strange dream! I simply dismissed it and went back to sleep.

The next night I had the exact same dream. And a third time, I had it during a nap that afternoon.

"*Ok Lord, you have my attention,*" I thought. By the fourth time, in my dream state I tried to pay attention to any details I may have missed. I observed that I was laying on my side at His feet, curled up in a fetal position the way that I do when I either sleep or when I feel ill. I also noticed that in each dream I wasn't necessarily worshipping Him like Mary at His feet in Luke 10:39; I was actually incredibly *self-conscious* in each dream, which is why I was curled up. I wrote down these details in my journal and went about attending my Prophetic Summit.

The Sunday after the Summit had ended, I was having a restful time in God's presence, when suddenly I was taken into a waking vision – not a sleeping dream – where I literally saw the feet of Jesus before me. No longer was I sitting on the edge of my bed, I was now laying on my side at His feet. I had this nagging feeling of anxiety, like something was not right. The feeling was not discernment about the vision itself or a situation outside the vision – the feeling was about *me*. I was not sure what to do with it all, so I tried to pull myself up at least to His knees, but saw that the vision only went as high as His shins. And then suddenly, I was back sitting on the corner of my bed in my little, earthly reality again.

I grabbed my journal and Bible and began to

ask God what this was about. My first thought was the story about the woman who had the issue of blood, from Matthew 9:20–22 (also Mark 5:25–34, Luke 8:43–48). I read through the very familiar scripture and wondered to myself if perhaps there was some need or issue in my life where I was neglecting to act and "reach out and touch Jesus." After all, I have always identified with the woman in these passages. Not just regarding her contending for healing (which is a place that I have certainly been), but also because she was considered an outcast by her people due to her issue. It took a lot of courage to push through the crowds and come to Jesus the way she did, with the particular issue that she had. Rather than listening to the Holy Spirit on what HE was trying to say to me, I just assumed that I had some big issue that required His attention and I needed to throw myself at His feet and ask for healing. I searched my heart quickly (which is code for: I fished around for something wrong with me – which as I mentioned in a previous chapter is not the healthy thing to do), until I heard a loud voice in my Spirit. It was so loud inside of me that I thought for a second it was audible. I heard Him say to me to stop what I was doing and just turn to John 1.

A healthy fear of God came over me in that moment as I quieted myself under the weight of

His majesty and with shaking hands flipped the pages forward to the first chapter of John. Before I could even start at the top, my eyes immediately fell upon John 1:12-13, which reads: *"But to all who did receive him, who believed in his name, he gave the right **to become children of God**, who were born, not of blood nor of the will of the flesh nor of the will of man, but of God."*

Suddenly I heard the Father's voice correct me with such great love. When He corrects, He ALWAYS realigns us to truth. He said to me firmly, *"**Do you see this, Mandy? You are a DAUGHTER of the Most High, and you have been behaving like a woman with an issue. You are no longer a woman with an issue – now get up and face me...and start believing in your identity! There is nothing wrong with you.**"*

He Called Me Daughter

Here is the gist of what happened to the woman with the issue of blood from the Bible. Jesus is in a large crowd; the woman is desperate for healing. This woman is considered "unclean," and an "outcast" – unwanted, unloved, and with some big issues. She believes that Jesus is the man who can help her so she goes into the crowd, touches just the hem of His robe, and He feels power leave His body. He asks who touched Him and she makes her way to Him, throwing herself at His feet and explaining her story. Jesus looks at her and in Luke 8:48 He says to her, "*Daughter, your faith has healed you. Go in peace and be freed from your suffering*" (NIV).

The part I want to focus on is that Jesus calls her "*Daughter*". The Greek word that He uses here is the word ***thygatēr***[1] which literally means "*daughter of God; one acceptable to God*". This caught my attention and with the help of my Greek scholar husband, I began to journey through the gospels and look at every time Jesus spoke directly to a woman. What we found interesting is that every face-to-face encounter that Jesus had with a woman – even Mary and Martha and His own mother – He always referred to them directly as "Woman" (the Greek word ***gynē***,[1] which literally means a female). This woman who reached out to touch the robe of the great Healer is the only woman in scripture that I could find that Jesus directly called "Daughter" (and this has recently been confirmed, at the writing of the second publication of this book, by the powerful program called "The Chosen" – S3E5). I believe that this is significant for us, because she came to Jesus with all her issues and yet He chose to not only heal her, but give her a new IDENTITY.

The woman was indeed full of faith. She was courageous and probably at the end of her rope. Some passages say that she had used up all of her money to find healing, so she must have been poor, an outcast, afraid, probably also anxious and weary. Yet He called her DAUGHTER. Not just because of her faith or courage, but because when you come to Jesus in faith, touch His robe and let Him speak to you, He will always change your identity and place value upon you.

I am not a person with an issue, and neither are you if you are born-again. Your new identity is that you are a child of God, one with a new nature and an entirely new identity in Christ. It is a lie to believe that you belong only at the feet of Jesus, groveling for His healing – even if you do it with great faith. If you still struggle with believing these lies, ask Holy Spirit to speak to your heart as you re-read the previous few chapters. You are a new creation in Christ, dead to sin and alive to God in Christ Jesus. You have a righteous nature, and holiness is the fruit of your righteousness and intimacy with Him. He wants to remind you of who you truly are, and that there is nothing wrong with you. Do not remain at His feet in a groveling position – get up and gaze into His eyes.

Going Low Because You're a Child

Heidi Baker is a hero of mine in the faith. I have never met her, though I have heard her speak on numerous occasions. One thing that Heidi talks about often is "*going low*," and surrendering our "*little lives*" all to Him. Heidi can say this because she KNOWS that she is a daughter. If you hear her testimony, Heidi has been made fully alive in the knowledge of what Jesus has done and who He is to her, and therefore who *she is in Him*. Heidi spends most of her life walking hand-in-hand with her Jesus, gazing into His loving, powerful eyes to get all she needs. Thus, when Heidi says to "*go low*," it is not because she is groveling at His feet like a woman with an issue; it is because Heidi is so aware of her identity as Daughter that she *cannot help* but worship Him and wipe His feet with her most precious gift – **herself**.

Heidi is a Mary at the feet of Jesus. Identity comes from intimacy with Him, not from doing works *for* him. Good works flow once identity is established. Identity is established once a deep intimacy takes root. It all flows together.

I believe that Mary *simply wanted Jesus*. She *needed* Jesus. Mary did not sit at His feet because she was *striving* to be submissive, or *trying* to be obedient, or *groveling with issues* to be solved. She was not hoping to make a statement about her gender or oppression. She did not even sit there because she was wanting to glean some sort of knowledge about the scriptures. What Mary gained from sitting at the feet of Jesus *was Jesus Himself*, which is why He told her sister that she had chosen the "*good part*" (Luke 10:42, NASB)[2].

Mary knew she was a Daughter.

We have gained Jesus Himself. When we understand the magnitude of this truth, we will burn for nothing else BUT Him. It is who we were born-again to be. It is the reason for our freedom.

Who You Are

You are no longer a person with an issue. He calls you DAUGHTER. He calls you SON. He calls you FRIEND. He has made you NEW. When you know the true substance of your salvation, you will stop seeing yourself as a *"person with an issue!"* Seeing yourself in this way – with a whole new identity – changes everything. One of the most powerful moments in my life was when He spoke to me and said that I was no longer a person with an issue but a child of God, and His daughter. Knowing that I have full access to Him and that I can look Him straight in the face without shame has enabled me to look at Him *all the time*, and not just when I feel "worthy" enough. I AM worthy because of Jesus!

When you see yourself as a child who is adored and not a broken heap of disappointment, you will go so deep into places of intimacy with Him such as you could never have imagined! He is waiting to show you so much more of Himself. It is in that secret place with Him that you will continue to remember how truly free indeed He has made you!

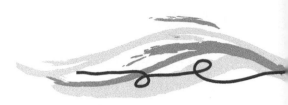

Chapter 7
Behold the Meadow

My heart burns for Jesus. Plain and simple. And my heart has burned brighter since understanding these truths and allowing them to take root in my heart and consume my thoughts. This depth of intimacy, even with God, has been confronting at times, yet I have decided to always push deeper and not turn back. He has challenged me many times to push in as far as I can and not just linger, but to not come out at all until I am released. The deeper I go, the more my heart burns for Him. I am learning the true meaning of *abiding* in His Presence.

"Abide" has been a cliché word for me in the past, and I have not fully understood it. The Apostle John loves to use the word "abide" in his gospel (John 15) as well as his three letters. If you look up this word abide in the Strong's concordance (S3306...thank you www. blueletterbible.org), it means a number of beautiful things. *To tarry, not to depart, to continue to be present, to be held, to remain as one, to last or endure, to wait for*

– just to name a few. Does this imagery not make your heart leap? I get hungry for more of Him when I read what abide actually means.

At the time of writing the first release of this book, since understanding that I am truly free indeed, I no longer struggle through seasons of "dryness" or "numbness." I have found that if I do start to feel any sense of numbness to the glory or presence of God, it is always because I have made a choice to agree with a lie about myself. Yet thankfully through the knowledge of my true identity, the power of those lies is now easily broken. My seasons of "numbness" now last only minutes as opposed to weeks, months or years. My ability to prophetically hear the Father's voice is keener, my taste for the supernatural is heightened, and my desire for holiness and purity has never been so great. I just love to abide.

I have definitely found that there is a direct correlation between remembering who I am and my quantity and quality time in His presence. The revelation of my righteous nature actually fuels my hunger for His presence more than ever. I burn for Him because of what He did for me, and then when I connect with Him, I remember that what He went through for me to transform me into a woman who is free indeed. This makes me want to throw myself at His feet more and more in reverence, worship and adoration. It changes my desires and longings, and it aligns my heart and thoughts to His. It is a beautiful place of intimacy that I had not been able to find in all my years of being saved. I also have a love for the Bible that I never would have imagined for myself. As my friend Mark Greenwood says, the word is a mirror not a measure.[1] And it is in His Presence and His Word that we see just how much we look like our Father.

The Meadow

Years ago, after a season of great endurance and some pain, Carston and I moved back to Sydney, Australia where we found healing at a beautiful church called Jubilee Church. During a healing service one day, I was laid out on the cold floor just soaking up His presence, when suddenly, I found myself feeling grass beneath me. *I literally felt grass*, and when I opened my eyes, I found myself not on a cement floor in Sydney, but in a large, green, lush meadow! I had entered the most powerful waking vision (or trance?) in my life to date. There were all of my favorite wildflowers in full bloom: Bright red poppies, crocus, yellow-bells, wisteria, and more. The trees were tall and had brilliantly vivid leaves and were easy to climb, much like the live oak trees in my home in South Louisiana. The sunshine was bright but not too warm or blinding, and there was a peaceful, babbling brook near this spot in the meadow where I found myself. I could still hear the worship music in the background, and it felt as if the music was the theme song to my supernatural experience.

After some time of picking wildflowers and chasing little frogs through the mud like a child, I saw a figure approach me from across the meadow. At first, he was just a silhouette in the bright sunshine, but as He approached and my heart began to pound, I knew it was Jesus! Jesus came toward me with a huge smile and adoring eyes, and He grabbed my arm and spun me around like a gentleman about to whisk away a lady for a dance. We actually danced and laughed together for a time, just enjoying being together. This is a memory that is more vivid and real to me at times than even my own wedding.

I spent what felt like hours in the meadow with Jesus and I felt more than refreshed, but I could hear that the meeting was ending and someone was offering up a closing prayer. I remember anxiety begin to rise in me again, and I hid my face tightly in Jesus' chest, begging for Him to not make me go back. I loved my husband and my friends and family but I was *so, so tired* and even angry. I knew that I could never again face the busy, striving kind of life of ministry we had been living, although I was certain that I had a calling on my life. I also felt like a failure, and was ready to just lay down and accept that I was indeed one. Had I missed something in my walk? Did I somehow step out of some kind of anointing that was supposed to carry me through? Was I too selfish or broken to be able to build the kingdom properly? Were past leaders correct when they said that I was not cut out for ministry?

All of these questions raced through my mind when Jesus gently touched my chin and lifted my eyes up toward His. He said to me these words that have forever been burned into my heart and soul: *"You were created to minister from this meadow, this place of rest and enjoyment...you were never created to strive or do any of this in your own strength...you were created **for** the meadow **with Me**. Everything you do comes from the meadow. It is part of who you are in ME."*

When I opened my eyes, the meeting had finished and the room had almost completely cleared out. A few of my friends who lingered around afterward said it looked as if I was in a trance from the moment the music started until it ended. One friend said she sensed God's presence and glory all over me, and she saw a physical change in my countenance as well! I have not since experienced anything quite like this encounter. It has had layers of meaning for me over the years, and I am still learning from this beautiful experience. My first book, "Daughter in the Meadow," describes this encounter in more detail, and documents the first of my revelations of what the meadow is for a believer.

We Each Have a Meadow

I do **not** believe that God has reserved this meadow experience for only a few special people. My encounter looks vastly different to my husband's, which looks vastly different to yours. The meadow was significant to my life at that time because I had just come out of a season of busyness and striving. At that time in my life, I thought that I was a failure in ministry and I still believed that I was just a "sinner saved by grace" who was forgiven but never going to be completely free or good enough. This encounter planted seeds in my heart for my journey of finding out the true significance of what Jesus did for me. Many would call my meadow the "secret place," or simply, *abiding* in Him. Regardless of what you may call it, the point Jesus made is that *everything we do comes from this place – the meadow*. And the meadow is in us.

There are places of intimacy that I am convinced can only be found by those who have understood that they are transformed sons and daughters of God with new natures. Some people may act like orphans who feel they have to clean up, dress up and act accordingly in order to be accepted or loved by God and man. But those who have died with Christ know that they are also approved of by Him. This allows them to rest and lean into Him, enjoying life without striving for fear of not obeying Him or somehow missing the mark.

Righteousness is an open door to intimacy. You enter the door *by faith*, and you push into intimacy. A righteous person knows that they are acceptable to God, so they are able to enter the inner courts with Him because this space has been made available to them. Because of faith in Jesus and your new nature, you can actually enjoy God. You can minister to HIS heart!

Whether it is dancing in a meadow, chasing little frogs in the mud or laying at His feet in complete adoration, it is all yours. It is who you are. It is an overflow from your righteous heart. It is part of your redeemed original design.

You Were Made for This

You look like Jesus, if indeed Jesus is inside of you. The more you behold Him in your own meadow, the more He reminds you of just how much you look like Him, which makes you start to act like

Him. It is not a matter of *doing* (getting into your "quiet time" out of obligation); it is a matter of believing and just *being* the crucified, transformed, born-again, righteous and holy son or daughter that you are! When you allow Him to love on you and remind you of yourself, then everything you do from there is a true *love response*, meaning *everything you do comes from your meadow.*

As for me, because I am innocent I will see your face until I see you for who you really are. Then I will awaken with your form and be fully satisfied, fulfilled in the revelation of your glory in me! – Psalm 17:15 (TPT)[2]

When I first got passionate about Jesus in my late teens, going into my secret place was only an obligatory event that occurred because I was afraid of letting God down. It was something good that I "should" do often because that is what good Christians do. But soon a passion grew in me, and I moved from *obligation to need.* I feel like need is unfortunately where a lot of believers stay. Let me clarify: Knowing our need for His presence is a *really good thing*! He provides grace, rest, comfort, identity, even power. In fact, I used to not go out and do any type of ministry until I was "prayed up," because only then I knew my need for Him and my reliance on His Spirit and not my flesh. Those are GOOD things! ***But our intimacy with Jesus goes beyond our need.***

He redeemed us for **relationship**. Otherwise, we would just be kingdom-building robots that plug into a power source for a while then rush off to do good works. Remember, abiding, according to the Apostle John (and the Strong's Concordance), means *being held* and *remaining as one*. This is true intimacy.

Do not miss the whole point of your righteousness my friend: You have been made *righteous* in nature for *relationship* with your Father. You are not approved of and compatible with Him just for yourself. He loved you first and chose you for HIMSELF. This is the highest goal of intimacy, to be able to look deeply into the eyes of your loved one and say, "*I am my beloved's and my beloved is mine*" (Song of Solomon 6:3). To be fully known and seen and loved by one another is the most glorious part of any relationship.

The meadow is part of who I am because it is the meeting place of myself and my Beloved. It is so deep for me now that I carry it around inside of me. My new nature allows me to go deeper and deeper in every time. It is my favorite place ever. And all it takes is faith to enter in, again and again and again, whenever I desire.

I believe that the following passage from Song

of Songs (2:11-13) in the Passion Translation is a prophetic declaration over the Bride as she begins to know her identity and thus push deeper into her meadow (I made some portions bold, for emphasis). I nearly weep whenever I read these words from the bride-groom to His bride. I will let the words speak for themselves:

*The season has changed, the **bondage of your barren winter has ended**, and the season of **hiding** is over and gone. The rains have soaked the earth and left it bright with blossoming flowers. The season for singing and pruning the vines has arrived. I hear the cooing of doves in our land, filling the air with **songs to awaken you** and guide you forth. **Can you not discern this new day of destiny breaking forth around you?** The early **signs of my purposes and plans** are bursting forth. The budding vines of new life are now blooming everywhere. The fragrance of their flowers whispers, "There is change in the air." **Arise, my love, my beautiful companion, and run with me to the higher place. For now is the time to arise and come away with me.**[2]*

Intimacy is everything. It is our LIFE. The whole reason that Jesus died was because we have a Father who is so desperately in love with us that He could not bear the thought of living without His beautiful ones. YOU ARE LOVED. This revelation will change everything, and this book would not exist without this conviction – which I have found for myself in my own "meadow."

Come Away, Free One

Remember, you are free indeed because you died with Him and now you are just like Him. You must find Him in your own secret place on a regular basis in order to keep your mind in agreement with the truth about Jesus (and you). As I mentioned before, the more you meet with Him in those secret places, the more your heart will burn for Him and the more He will go deeper with you. You will begin to desire Him and desire holiness in new ways, and you will begin to see that as you lean against His chest, you have the same heartbeat as the Father. And as you understand how intensely loved and valued you are, you will move into such a relationship with Him like you have never known!

You and I have to remember not to get so caught up in understanding and being and doing and spreading the love that we forget why we are actually free indeed in the first place. It is all for HIM. It is all for *relationship and intimacy*. Like Heidi Baker, you can throw yourself at His feet in adoration. Abide. Intimacy is always the goal.

Chapter 8
Engaging as a Bold Lion

The Church is awakening. She is about to ROAR. In fact, in 2020 as I finished the first manuscript, I was then hearing the true roars of this beautiful Bride. I feel it beginning to shift in my spirit so strongly, and with many others across the globe I have been prophetically interceding this awakening into being. Everything my eyes see, especially in nature, seems to prophetically point to it.

In 2017 my husband and I watched the solar eclipse right in the line of totality in South Carolina, USA. I have traveled the world and seen some amazing things in my life, but I am uncertain as to whether I have ever seen anything quite as awe-inspiring as this eclipse! The seconds leading up to totality felt as if everyone held their breath until that wonderful moment – and then as the moon covered the sun, I felt the earth and time itself stand still. Literally *everyone* in my vicinity took a giant, collective gasp at its beauty. I was in tears and overwhelmed at the goodness of Father God in that moment.

What I noticed more than anything in the 5-10 minutes leading up to totality was how creation responded. I even posted it on Facebook, asking if I was the only one experiencing this, and of course I was not. Bugs were marching in circles in the grass at our feet. Birds were dive-bombing trees in excitement. Dogs were barking and leaping around in the park where we watched. As the eerie darkness began to close in just before totality, cicadas began to sing this stunning melody and birds were in tune with even the cicadas. That in itself was beautiful for those that had ears to hear and paid attention to it.

After the eclipse had passed, friends were responding on social media with phrases like, "*This is the most glorious thing I have ever witnessed,*" and "*I will never use the word 'awesome' again since nothing but Jesus compares to the solar eclipse.*" I even had an atheist friend comment, "*This sort of thing almost makes me believe there is a God...*" Days later, people were still overwhelmed by its beauty and glory and obsessed with photos of the totality. Even months after, people were communicating about how the splendor of the eclipse made them feel, how it opened their eyes to "more" in life and the universe. Some even said that for a brief moment in America, amidst all the political turmoil and chaos, people looked UP at something other than themselves and their fears, and they stood in awe, unified.

I felt the Lord say to me just after the totality, that this is just a glimpse of His Church, and that humanity will say even GREATER things about the Church as she grows more glorious in her understanding of who she is!

"For I consider that the sufferings of this present time are not worthy to be compared with the glory that is to be revealed to us. For the anxious longing of the creation waits eagerly for the revealing of the sons of God." – Romans 8:18, 19

The Holy Spirit brought this scripture to mind when I heard the birds and bugs begin to sing just before totality. In the original Greek, when read in context, what Paul says here is that creation is waiting in suspense for the manifestation of those who are born-again to grasp and understand, by the Spirit, how great are the benefits of salvation (thank you blueletterbible.com). The "revealing" of the sons of God – some translations say the "manifestation" of the sons – simply means that the Children of God (the Bride) will rise up in glory because by faith they finally understand their righteousness and beauty! *"He made Him who knew no sin to be sin on our behalf, so that we might become the righteousness of God in Him."* – 2 Corinthians 5:21 (NASB).

This is an important season in which the Church's eyes are opening to a great revelation of her identity. I believe there will be a time when, like the solar eclipse, humanity will gasp in awe at the beauty of the Church when by faith she becomes fully aware of who she is. We will be moved to see the goodness of Father God when we begin seeing His goodness in ourselves and what He did for us. People will be in awe of the Church as she rises up to take her rightful place. She will be so glorious in these coming days that *even those who do not know our God will be drawn to Him* – she will be the very thing of beauty that makes man rethink where he stands with God. She will not bring condemnation but salvation and *transformation* because as she rises up, she will carry the Spirit of the Living God within her, and when Jesus is lifted up, He promises He will draw all men unto Himself (John 12:32). She will know that she is no longer a "woman with an issue," but she will be so convicted of her righteous nature (John 16:8) that she will burn for intimacy with her Jesus and as a mirror she will reflect the glory of God to the nations.

But we all, with unveiled face, beholding as in a mirror the glory of the Lord, are being transformed into the same image from glory to glory, just as from the Lord, the Spirit. – 2 Corinthians 3:18 (NASB)[1]

The Devil Hates Bold Lions

The righteous are as bold as lions – Proverbs 28:1

I asked God about two years ago WHY. Why have I only been taught half-truths about my identity? Why have I never, until recently, had the understanding or language to see that I have a righteous, new, transformed nature? Why have I never been told that sin is now external to me and that I truly do have freedom? God's answer was so simple: ***"Because the righteous are as bold as lions, and the devil doesn't want Christians to be bold."***

Think about it. The devil is rejected, without hope, without peace and he hates anything that looks like Jesus – and that, my friend, is YOU. If he can keep you in bondage, thinking you are forever bound to whatever you struggle with, then you will *never be bold for Jesus because you will never know that you can be.* He wants you to be like Adam and Eve, believing the lies that you are lacking something and cannot look fully like Jesus until you get to Heaven. LIES!

I am also passionate about equipping the saints to share their faith. I do not necessarily consider myself to have the Billy Graham or Reinhard Bonnke ascension gift of "evangelist," but I actively share my faith and have been graced to teach and equip others how to do it without fear or shame.

One of the strategies that the Lord has given me is answering one deep question: **Why is Jesus worth dropping everything to follow?** I believe that if a believer can articulate, with conviction, why they have dropped everything to follow Jesus – then they can evangelize.

This question often blows the minds of my students because it forces them to really *think*. For some, the answer may be simple. "*Jesus set me free from addiction*" or "*Jesus invaded my world and brought peace when my relationship fell apart*" are valid answers. But what about those of us who have not had these experiences and feel like we have nothing "dramatic" to say? When accepting the truth that we are new creations in Christ, with a whole new nature, my articulation of this question changes drastically.

"*I once was living in darkness, suicidal and full of anxiety and sinful desires. Then I met Jesus, repented of my sins, and now I am full of light, full of peace and hope, I am no longer anxious about my future and I am a completely transformed woman with completely new desires.*" This is my personal testimony, and it is definitely relatable to many in today's world. Realizing what Jesus has actually done for me has given me something to share, more than the typical "Jesus wants to have a relationship with you" phrase that many use in evangelism. Yes, of course He wants to have a relationship with us, but most unsaved do not want to hear this because they either do not understand it, or they do not think that they are worthy enough for Jesus anyway. But knowing that they can be free and transformed – that draws them in because it speaks to their greatest need and desire. If you think about it, however, if you do not truly *believe* that you are free or a new creation, you will stay silent about it.

Knowing what Jesus *truly did for us* is a reason for the enemy to try his hardest to keep us silent and bound in shame and guilt. He does not want the truth about the reality of Jesus being more than just a ticket to Heaven going public.

Likewise, if the devil can keep you from finding your meadow – if he can keep you from intimacy with God because of the lies that you think or feel about yourself – then you will never fulfill the very reason that you were created: Deep, intimate, vulnerable **RELATIONSHIP with the Father**. And your relationship with the Father fuels your boldness for sharing Jesus.

I am not overly "extroverted," as the world would call it, but I love to share Jesus with the lost because it is a response in my heart to knowing just how free and found in Him that I am. Now that I know it, it is hard for me to not share because I know intimately why Jesus is worth dropping everything to follow.

The devil is crafty and will do whatever he can to keep you from relationship, keep you in lies and keep you from walking in holiness and the boldness for fulfilling the great commission. He will keep you shut down, feeling condemned and stressed, feeling rejected and left out and defeated. And all of these things keep you from intimacy with God and with man.

What a liar!

Don't Engage

Can you see why knowing and believing the truth about our salvation is so important? We must learn to only engage with truth in these days. Let me share a story from my daily life that will paint a better picture.

A previous neighbor who lived across the road from us in the USA used to have issues with his three big dogs getting out of his fenced yard and running up and down the street. The dogs were rambunctious, would bark at people and would chase cars. They were intimidating and even the postal workers would carry sticks to be sure they were safe.

One day a man was walking down the street, and the dogs were out. They ran up and down the street along the opposite side of the road to him, barking and snarling and jumping around.

However, the man kept his eyes fixed in front of him and did not flinch. After a moment, the dogs got no response from the man, so they backed off and the man continued his journey, dog free.

That same afternoon, a woman was walking along and the dogs started acting up again. The difference is that the woman *engaged the dogs*. Where the man kept walking and never made eye-contact, the woman looked straight at the dogs and started yelling swear words at them. She picked up a stick from our yard and went to throw it at them, but the dogs charged at her and knocked her over. The story ends with me calling 911 and the woman crying hysterically.

The Lord really used this situation to teach me a valuable lesson about the lies of the enemy in my own life. How many times in the past had I engaged the intimidation, fear and accusations of the devil? It is such a trap, because the result was the same every time – there was always pain and I would always feel overcome. Yet, if I had not even acknowledged the junk that the enemy was whispering to me and just kept my eyes on the truth about God and the truth about me, I would have saved myself years of grief and pain.

Friend, when the accuser of the brethren comes to tell you that all of the truth you have learned about Jesus and the substance of your salvation is bogus, you *must* be like the gentleman walking down my road and ***not engage***. Remember the truth and only allow that truth to enter your mind. Do not dwell, even for a second, on the devil's innuendos. He is a father of lies and there is absolutely ZERO truth in Him (John 8:44). Let us look at how Jesus does it in Matthew 4:1-11:

And the tempter came and said to Him, "If you are the Son of God, command these stones to become loaves of bread." But He answered, "It is written, "Man shall not live by bread alone, but by every word that comes from the mouth of God." Then the devil took Him to the holy city and set Him on the pinnacle of the temple and said to Him, "If you are the Son of God, throw yourself down, for it is written, 'He will command His angels concerning you,' and 'On their hands they will bear you up, lest you strike your foot against a stone.' "Jesus said to him, "Again it is written, 'You shall not put the Lord your God to the test.'" Again, the devil took Him to a very high mountain and showed Him all the kingdoms of the world and their glory. And he said to Him, "All these I will give you, if you will fall down and worship me." Then Jesus said to him, "Be gone, Satan! For it is written, 'You shall worship the Lord your God and him only shall you serve.' "Then the devil left Him, and behold, angels came and were ministering to Him.

I believe that Jesus is the perfect example of one who did not engage with the devil! The devil came to Him and tried to bring intimidation, but Jesus only responded with *truth*. Jesus never once engaged, yelled at the devil or even tried to debate him. Jesus spoke truth until the devil left Him alone. And in doing this, Jesus taught us a better way than Adam and Eve had chosen. *"For we do not have a high priest who is unable to sympathize with our weaknesses, but one who in every respect has been tempted as we are, yet without sin"* (Hebrews 4:15).

Whom the Son sets free is free indeed – John 8:36

Thanks to Jesus, the only truth you need engage with is the truth about HIM. As He is, so are you. You have been restored to original design in Him. You are as righteous as Him. Holy living is an overflow of your relationship with Him. You are not an orphan, but a son or daughter who has full access to your Heavenly Father. You were made in His image, with His characteristics and His Holy Spirit to remind you how loved you are. The Bible says that you are a partaker of His divine nature (2 Peter 1:4), and you are seated with Christ in Heavenly places (Ephesians 2:6). Colossians 3:2 says to set your mind on things above, not on earthly things.

Know these truths, and the truth will set you free (John 8:32). Engage only these truths about yourself, and the devil will have to back down. Do not fall into the trap of his innuendos. He is such a liar and he is crafty.

I believe the helmet of salvation mentioned in Ephesians 6 is simply putting on, or engaging with, the TRUTH about what your salvation truly looks like. In this way, I often use my truth helmet as an offense weapon and not a defense weapon. The fact that you are free and transformed completely on the inside is one of the greatest truth weapons that God has given us.

Yes, you are free indeed.

Are you ROARING yet???

Chapter 9
Strongholds in the Mind

In the previous chapter, I talked about learning to not engage the lies of the enemy. One of the greatest lessons I have learned over the years is that when a lie, or a lying feeling comes up, I do not even give it the time of day. I know how imperative it is to not partner with anything other than what God says about myself, about Him, or about my new nature in Christ.

But what about strongholds, you may ask. A stronghold, as per one definition, is *a place where a particular cause or belief is strongly defended or upheld.*[1] The word used for "stronghold" in 2 Corinthians 10:4 is the word **ochyrōma**, which means a fortress, but also "*…of the arguments and reasoning by which a disputant endeavors to fortify his opinion and defend it against his opponent.*[2]

For the weapons of our warfare are not of the flesh but have divine power to destroy strongholds – 2 Corinthians 10:4

Here is what the Lord showed me about a stronghold: **A stronghold is a fortress that builds up in a person's mind as they repeatedly engage with lies, and it seeks to fortify the lies that the person has partnered with.** In other words, the more I engage the enemy's lies about my identity and whether I am free or not, the more the enemy has access to build up a sort of fortress in my mind that can only be demolished by Heavenly weapons of warfare.

We destroy arguments and every lofty opinion raised against the knowledge of God, and take every thought captive to obey Christ, being ready to punish every disobedience, when your obedience is complete. Look at what is before your eyes. If anyone is confident that he is Christ's, let him remind himself that just as he is Christ's, so also are we. – 2 Corinthians 10:5-7

As a born-again daughter of the Most High, I have learned to grab ahold of a lie the minute it appears (most of the time). I believe the Father wants to teach us to become good at knowing when it is a lie or a lying feeling. Regardless of how real the thought or emotion appears, if it is opposite to what scripture says or what the Father has already spoken, then it is NOT TRUTH.

As the Body of Christ, we are in a bible revival season of knowing what the Word says, and learning to stand on the truth that we read. This is also where intimacy comes in again, and our ability to hear from the Father for ourselves and know just how incredibly loved and approved of we are. The more we abide in Him – in His love, in His approval, in His rest and hearing His heartbeat – the more we are able to resist the lies that the enemy tries to throw at us to cause us to fall prey to sin.

Taking the Thoughts Captive

Learning to take our thoughts captive is a bit different to renewing our minds in His love. We renew our minds by digging into His Word, and allowing His presence to wash over us with His affirmation and the truth about who we truly are. Taking thoughts captive, on the other hand, is learning to grab the lie before we fully engage with it, and making it immediately submit to Jesus.

The Holy Spirit wants to teach you individually to do this, but I am happy to share with you how I take thoughts captive, so that you at least have a starting point if this is new to you. I also would like to add, once again, that additional help is always available for those who have had to live life with what I call a "scaffolding" up around yourself due to past traumas or too many years of engaging with the lies of the enemy. Seeking help to dismantle these structures does not negate the truth that you are a new creation in Christ, who has a new nature and has been restored to Him completely. Getting help to understand these truths is healthy, and it means that the Holy Spirit is at work to see you manifesting the freedom that is already yours because of Christ Jesus.

When taking thoughts captive, I do this personally by grabbing the lie or the lying emotion and I literally imagine myself balling it up in my fist, *separating it from myself,* and dropping it at the feet of Jesus. It is almost as if I can see all the lies and all the hurt the lies want to cause (or have caused) being smashed to bits at His feet! I see these things in pieces at His feet, and I then ask the Holy Spirit to remind me who I am, how the Father feels about me, and how Jesus Himself sees me. Jesus never fails to show up and defeat those lies with His ever-lasting truths.

Often if I have engaged with the lies a bit before I bring it to Him, I use that time to repent of partnering with those lies and I begin to speak aloud truths about myself. In this process of speaking truth aloud, what I am doing is building my faith (faith comes by hearing – Romans 10:17), and I am allowing my mind and emotions to catch up with what my Spirit already knows to be true about me. Sometimes this may take a bit of time, especially if I have allowed the lies to build up like plaque around my heart. But I use self-control to keep a strong grip on my spirit, and I continue to lean into His truth so that there is no room for the enemy to continue his lies.

A man without self-control is like a city broken into and left without walls. – Proverbs 25:28

In this process, I can almost always feel a shift in the atmosphere around me, and I usually walk away feeling complete peace and extreme clarity again.

Using Your Helmet as a Weapon

The Lord showed me a silly picture for my friend Ben once, which I would love to share with you because I feel it is actually a tool to help people learn to fight the lying thoughts and feelings with their Spiritual weapons instead of worldly philosophies.

I looked over at my friend Ben one day, and I immediately saw everything in the natural turn into a cartoon. I am a prophetic seer, so I was not surprised by this manifestation, although I had never seen the world through cartoon eyes before!

When I looked over at Ben, I saw that he had the full armor of God on his body (Ephesians 6), and he was swinging the sword of the Spirit like he was ready to cut off the head of a giant. I saw a sneaky demon coming toward Ben, and while he was going after it with his sword, he did not see that there was another, larger demonic force approaching his head, unnoticed, from above.

What I saw next was both hilarious as well as profound: As soon as Ben had killed the demon in front of him with his sword, he quickly turned to the sneaky demon above him and he *headbutted the demon with his helmet of salvation*! The demon was headbutted a few times before it was defeated, but when it disappeared, I knew it was indeed gone. Soon the cartoon encounter ended, and Ben was hugely encouraged by what I saw!

Perhaps, like me, you have always been told that the helmet of salvation is actually a defensive weapon used to cover the mind, or used to protect the mind or thoughts of the believer. I am not totally disagreeing with this teaching, but I would also like to propose that when the enemy begins to throw lying thoughts at us as believers, we have every right to take the helmet and begin to use it as an offensive weapon!

As it is the helmet of *salvation*, once we know the true substance of our salvation and the fact that we are truly free indeed, we can fight off the enemy by using what we know about our salvation to not just protect our thoughts, but to conquer every lie that the accuser tries to throw at us. I believe that working with the sword, the shield, and all the bits of the armor, we can stand even more victorious when we know what the helmet of salvation actually means to us. Just like trade workers tend to use a protective helmet while standing on scaffolding, I believe that we can use our helmet of salvation to help us *demolish the scaffolding* that we often build against the knowledge of what Jesus has done for us!

Rewriting the Negative Thoughts

At the time of the first manuscript, as I was pondering if I should even include this chapter, the home we lived in was having some major landscaping done. One side of the house did not have a gate or fence, and there were ruts in the dirt where vehicles had been driven regularly down the path to park in the back. At one stage, I noticed that the ruts in the dirt were changing location as wheels were being driven over and over the same area during the landscaping. What was happening was that a new "groove" in the ground was being written, and the old ruts in the dirt were starting to disappear completely *as they were not being used as regularly.* There was a moment before the completion of the project where I felt the Holy Spirit say to me, "*This is how I rewrite the negative thoughts and strongholds you have had in your mind."*

Wow. What an image.

Let us look at this in the context of thought patterns that we have built. If we have engaged with lies and allowed strongholds to build up, our thoughts will automatically go down the previously driven routes because that is what we are used to. I remember when we first moved to the home previously mentioned, any wheels that would go down that dirt path alongside the house would automatically drop into the already visible ruts in the ground, mostly because that was easier than driving along a bumpy ground that had no real pathway.

Likewise, if a person has engaged enough with negative thoughts, it will become a *counterfeit default* – and thus *feel* as if it is reality simply because it has been the default for so long.

Yet someone who now understands they are free indeed will know the truth as *the only reality*. Even if the counterfeit default feels more "natural" at first, all it takes is consistent rewriting of thought patterns by choosing to *go another route* in thinking. Taking the lies captive, giving them to Jesus, declaring the truth and choosing to not engage the lies anymore is a great start to digging new "ruts" in the pathways of our thoughts.

I believe that a stronghold on the mind is

broken by engaging *only the truth*, repenting of partnership with lies and closing any doors or breaches where the lies can legally get in, and then consistently rewriting new pathways in thinking. I am also convinced that this only happens through intimacy and friendship with the Father, reliance on His grace and the empowering of the Holy Spirit, and an expectation and faith in what has already been accomplished for you by Jesus.

Sometimes we need the help of a trusted friend, a counselor or inner healing minister to identify these ruts in our thinking, help us dismantle the lies and rebuild in truth. As long as we remember that the truth about us is that the identity that Jesus died to give us is a son or daughter who is FREE, we can approach these situations without shame. We are not people with issues, we just need a bit of help smashing the devil in the face sometimes!

Prayer to Engage With

If you have struggled in the past with negative thought patterns, engaging the lies or struggling to shake off the lying emotions, please remember that condemnation and guilt are ILLEGAL in your life because you are the righteousness of God in Christ Jesus (Romans 8:1). If you have repented and confessed your sins to your loving Father, not only are your sins forgiven and you are cleansed from all unrighteousness (1 John 1:9), but you also now have no legal ground for the enemy to stand on.

To begin forming new pathways and defaults in your thinking, I would suggest you read this prayer aloud in your time with the Lord, and then spend time marinating in the truth that Jesus did it all *for you*. Take that helmet of salvation and smash the devil in the face! May the truth that you are free indeed be your new default!

Precious Jesus, I thank you for what you did so that I could walk in freedom. I confess that I have engaged with lies and partnered with the following lies:_____. I repent of agreeing with the lies of the accuser, and I accept the truth that by faith in Jesus I am truly free indeed! By my repentance, I close the door to all legal access that the enemy has had through my partnership with these lies. I thank you again for freedom, for joy, for peace and for the righteousness of God in Christ Jesus that now resides in me. Amen.

Chapter 10
Time to Roar

What a journey we have been on! If you are anything like me, you may need to take some time to pray, process and seek the scriptures for yourself. In fact, I encourage you to do so! The Bible says to examine the scriptures daily and with great eagerness (Acts 17:10-11, NASB)[1]. You may feel a bit confused, but remember that God is not the author of confusion (1 Corinthians 14:33). Simply ask the Holy Spirit to reveal all truth to you.

Keep in mind that you may have to *unlearn* some things, like I did. You may have to be consistent with rewriting the path that your thoughts take. You may need to repent of the lies that you have partnered with. But above all, you may need to just sit and let the Father lavish His love upon you. Sit with Him, and do not pull away until He releases you – He has got so much beauty to share. Intimacy with Him is why you were created, and the key to unlocking every revelation about freedom that you long for.

Don't Feed the Old Man

Before we end our journey together, I wanted to share with you one last, powerfully confronting dream I had which I know will speak to you and perhaps tie some thoughts together.

In the dream, I was visiting and ministering to people who were struggling with different issues. Some were dealing with depression and anxiety, some with sickness, others with quite obvious sin such as lying and porn. None of these people were people that I knew in real life.

At the homes of each person whom I visited in the dream, there was an old man lingering around. Each home had the same situation – a struggle, and an old man who barely engaged the family, but who was just simply there. In one home that I went into, I decided to confront the old man and ask him about himself. He never gave me a direct answer about his identity, but the general sense I got from him was that he was negative, sickly, stressed and ashamed.

I remember him clearly telling me that he was "*allowed to stay*" by the person, and that he "*wasn't leaving until they said to go.*" When I spoke to the person about what the old man had said to me, they had a similar reaction. "*He seems harmless – I have learned to just tolerate him*" the person said of the old man. I noticed that each person had been feeding and housing their old man as well.

As the dream progressed, I ran into a friend whom I knew in real life as a highly spiritually discerning individual. She and I saw one another just outside of one of the homes I was visiting, and as she caught a glimpse of the old man lingering around the house, she made note that there was "*something wrong*" with the old person being allowed to hang around. I agreed.

The dream them switched to my friend and I pushing deep into prayer together, and having a time of worship of our Jesus. As I went deeper and deeper into the Father's heart in this dream, my perspective changed. My heartbeat began to connect to His rhythm, and it was as if I had new eyes to see the world around me. This is what the meadow does.

Soon after coming out of my meadow time with Jesus, I looked over at the old man, and what I saw absolutely astounded me. It was horrifically confronting.

I saw that the old man was actually *not alive*, but a dead corpse that was rotting. The corpse was being used as a puppet by two demons. None of us had seen the old man for what he really was before because he had been tolerated to such a point it appeared as if he somehow belonged there. The demonic is always subject to what we allow.

Soon the Holy Spirit spoke to me about the corpse. The Holy Spirit said that the "old man" was *more than just a wrong mindset*. This was something that had been *tolerated, fed and housed*, and therefore could legally be used by demonic forces to keep people in a struggle.

This "old man" – this *old nature* – had been tolerated for so long that the people I was visiting had actually partnered with the lie that it was harmless. In doing so, they could no longer see the truth for what it was – that it was a *dead corpse* and just simply needed to be told to GO. They needed God's presence and His heartbeat to be able to see from His perspective the truth about who they are, and that they no longer needed that old man to hang around and influence their lives! What a profound dream.

Friends, let our focus be today that we have been *crucified with Christ*, and that *it is no longer we who live but Christ who lives in us!* Whom the Son sets free, is free indeed, and that includes freedom from that old man who tries to linger and lie to you. We no longer have an obligation to engage him, to allow him to linger or to house and feed him *because he no longer lives*. We can see him as dead, and thus illegal in our lives, and definitely NOT something to be tolerated!

You will know the truth, and the truth will set

you free (John 8:32), and that truth is that the old man is a lie. The fact is, if you feel that you have to tolerate him, that is a lie. The truth is that you have authority to tell the enemy to GO, in the Name of Jesus, and you have the ability to smash every lie that raises itself against the knowledge of who you truly are in Christ. Being free does not mean that lying spirits will not try to hang around and provoke us. But it does mean that we have everything we need to defeat the lies and remain strong in who we truly are. We will tolerate whatever we do not recognize, and we can only recognize the lies when the truth is louder and more visible. This happens in His presence, connected to His heart, and allowing His love and truth to wash over us. What a glorious place to abide!

Again, if you need help because the lies are so deeply rooted in your inner world, please reach out to a trusted counselor or minister. Freedom is your inheritance, and God graciously gives some the grace to help people get delivered of these demonic strongholds and walk in this freedom.

I am so excited to see a generation rising up who refuse to tolerate the old man. It is for freedom that He set us free (Galatians 5:1), which means our *freedom* will cause freedom in others. This is my prayer for anyone who reads this book.

The Lies Are Smashed

I have friends who have so completely received this truth by faith, that where they previously have needed years and hours of counseling, all they need now is a few minutes to disarm the lies and re-engage with truth before they quickly start walking in *complete* freedom again. "*Whom the Son sets free is free indeed*" (John 8:36). There is documented evidence of people now walking free from lust, free from addiction, free from pride, free from anger, free from extreme insecurity, free from homosexuality and porn, etc. because of the revelation of their righteousness in Christ Jesus. **You and the world around you cannot afford for you to *not get this*.** Jesus has TRANSFORMED YOU. You are no longer fighting your flesh to be free! You are alive to God in Christ Jesus and you simply have to receive this truth by faith. We must not forget that sin is a LIAR that has lost its power over your life because of what Jesus has done!

This is the time to encourage each other to never be stubborn or hardened by sin's deceitfulness – Hebrews 3:13, TPT

I also invite you to ask God to *encounter you* today. Your encounters and dreams may not look like mine, but I know that the Father's heart is to encounter you in new, fresh ways. I pray that you go deep into your own meadow with Him – which may actually also look like a porch swing, or a walk outdoors in nature, or a day at the beach, or an hour in your prayer closet, or something else – and in that place, allow Him to remind you that you are no longer a person with an issue. I promise as this revelation sinks in, you will find your heart burns for Jesus in ways you never knew possible and your "taste" for life and holiness will change drastically.

You have a fully transformed nature. You are no longer a person with issues but a *son or daughter*. You are completely *new* on the inside, *without sin in your DNA*. You are the righteousness of God in Christ Jesus. You are as bold as a lion. You are loved, approved of, and you have the Holy Spirit inside of you to guide, teach and empower you. You are not subject to your thoughts or emotions either – *everything* must submit to Christ in you, and He is the default for where your thoughts can land.

More than anything, you must believe that you have a beautiful Jesus who is so much greater than you could have ever imagined. Time to get to know Him and fall in love with Him all over again. Go into the meadow and let Him show you His heart….I will meet you there.

You are most certainly free indeed.

Invitation

"If I find in myself desires which nothing in this world can satisfy, the only logical explanation is that I was made for another world."
— C.S. Lewis, "Mere Christianity"[1]

Precious friend,

As we find ourselves at the end of this book, my prayer has been from day one of writing that Jesus become more real to you than ever. I have literally prayed over every page and asked Holy Spirit to reveal the God-truths to you that would set you free and make you more alive in Him than ever. I pray that you now understand that the substance of your salvation is more than a ticket to heaven and forgiveness.

I do know that some of you, however, may be wondering about this Jesus and how it is even possible to have the encounters with Him that I have had, and some of you may not understand the scriptures that we studied because you do not have a relationship with Jesus.

May I first say, these "encounters" and dreams and even the revelation of scripture are not just for *special people only*. I am special because of Who lives inside of me. I live this way because the Spirit of the Living God dwells within me (Romans 8:9; 1

Corinthians 3:16). This freedom and relationship with the Father is one that can only be reached through a personal, intimate relationship with Jesus Christ.

In the world, there are many roads that people travel to try and achieve peace or rest within themselves – but you must know that JESUS CHRIST is our only source of *true and lasting* peace and change (John 16:33; Philippians 4:7; Colossian 3:15; 2 Corinthians 5:17). This rest that we so long for in our souls can only come from knowing Jesus, walking with Jesus, and accepting Him as our only way to God and eternal life (John 3:16; Romans 3:23; Romans 5:12; Romans 10:9-10). In fact, God has promised this rest to His children as an inheritance (Hebrews 4).

The only way to finally live at peace with yourself and to be fully transformed and free is through Jesus. You will never be holy as He is holy (1 Peter 1:16) apart from faith in what Jesus did for you, and repentance for trying to do it all on your own without Him.

"..if you confess with your mouth the Lord Jesus and believe in your heart that God has raised Him from the dead, you will be saved. For with the heart one believes unto righteousness, and with the mouth confession is made unto salvation - Romans 10:9-10, NKJV

If you find that you have never invited Jesus to be the Lord of your life and have never confessed with your mouth that you trust Him and want Him in your life, then this next prayer is for you.

Jesus, I invite You to come into my heart and my life. I admit that I am a sinner and that I cannot change on my own. I believe that you died for me, and to set me free. I confess that I need You! I believe that You died as me and then rose again so that I can live a new and transformed life. I trust You as my Lord and Savior, and I thank You for giving me your nature and making me Your child. Thank You that You have a plan for my life as a righteous saint! Please help me to understand how much You love me. Fill me to overflowing with your Holy Spirit – may He come into my life in complete fullness. In Jesus' Name I ask these things, Amen.

And for greater understanding of your decision, or if you would like me to pray for you, please feel free to contact me and let me know that you've prayed this prayer. I would love to rejoice with you and answer any questions that you may have!

outrageoushopegirl@gmail.com

@MandyGWoodhouse

Appendix
For Further Study

- Awake to Righteousness, Mark Greenwood (2017)
- Romans Chapters 1-8
- The Nature of Freedom, Graham Cooke (2016)
- Romans 6, Winnie Coco Banov (2015)
- "Your Created Value" – teaching by Todd White, found on YouTube
- "Identity Crash Course" – teaching by Dan Mohler, found on YouTube
- Identity Truth Bombs, Mandy Woodhouse (2019)
- Daughter in the Meadow, Mandy Woodhouse (2019)

Endnotes

Chapter 1

1. All Scripture quotations are from The Passion Translation®. Copyright © 2017, 2018 by Passion & Fire Ministries, Inc. Used by permission. All rights reserved. ThePassionTranslation.com.
2. Beckenham, Matt. Eden's Blueprint (Australia, Truly Loved Media, 2022).

Chapter 2

1. Greenwood, Mark. Awake to Righteousness (Australia, Saints by Nature Publishing, 2017).

Chapter 3

1. shorturl.at/sJT16, accessed on blueletterbible.org 2/8/19.

Chapter 4

1. Greenwood, Mark. Awake to Righteousness (Australia, Saints by Nature Publishing, 2017).
2. All stories used with permission.

Chapter 5

1. Scripture quotations marked NKJV are taken from the New King James Version, Copyright © 1982 by Thomas Nelson. All rights reserved.
2. Strongs 4413.
3. www.biblechronologytimeline.com/

biblechronologytimeline7.htm, accessed on 2/12/19.

4. https://www.chabad.org/library/article_cdo/aid/112374/jewish/The-Prophet-Ezekiel.htm, accessed on 2/12/19.

5. Thomas Schreiner wrote a fabulous piece for the Gospel Coalition: https://www.thegospelcoalition.org/article/romans-7-does-not-describe-your-christian-experience/. Accessed 2/19/19.

6. Daniel Thompson, Bible Scholar: https://www.preteristarchive.com/1999_thompson_a-commentary-on-romans-713-25/. Accessed 2/19/19.

Chapter 6

1. Blue Letter Bible, s.v. "thygatēr" and "gynē" accessed September 5, 2017, shorturl.at/brFKL / and "prōtos" shorturl.at/puyW1 (blueletterbible.org)

2. Scripture quotations taken from the New American Standard Bible® (NASB), Copyright © 1960, 1962, 1963, 1968, 1971, 1972, 1973, 1975, 1977, 1995 by The Lockman Foundation. Used by permission. www.Lockman.org

Chapter 7

1. Quote used with permission.

2. All Scripture quotations are from The Passion Translation®. Copyright © 2017, 2018 by Passion & Fire Ministries, Inc. Used by permission. All

Chapter 8

1. Scripture quotations taken from the New American Standard Bible® (NASB), Copyright © 1960, 1962, 1963, 1968, 1971, 1972, 1973, 1975, 1977, 1995 by The Lockman Foundation. Used by permission. www.Lockman.org

Chapter 9

1. shorturl.at/irACR (Google Search)
2. shorturl.at/agquA (blueletterbible.org)

Chapter 10

1. Scripture quotations taken from the New American Standard Bible® (NASB), Copyright © 1960, 1962, 1963, 1968, 1971, 1972, 1973, 1975, 1977, 1995 by The Lockman Foundation Used by permission. www.Lockman.org

Invitation

1. Lewis, C.S. Mere Christianiy (HarperCollins, 2009), pg. 136.

About the Author

Mandy Woodhouse first and foremost a Daughter of the King.

A Hope-Filled Prophetic voice and lover of Jesus.

Wife, photographer, Author and writer, artist, traveler, adventurer.

Dreamer, speaker, encourager, prophetic intercessor.

Evangelist, passionate to teach others to share their faith too. She is a life TRANSFORMED by Jesus. He is her favorite subject.

Mandy loves to "chase away the birds" for people (Luke 8:5).

She is passionate to teach others to buy truth and not sell it (Proverbs 23:23).

Originally from Lafayette, Louisiana, Mandy currently resides in Australia with her amazing Aussie husband (Carston) and three miniature schnauzers (Frodo, Charlie Jane and Mr. Wigglesworth). Through Outrageous Hope, Mandy runs online courses in identity, prayer, and the prophetic and she burns to see the world awakened to the truth about both personal identity as well as Who Jesus truly is. Mandy is a regular contributor to the Elijah List and at times Spirit Fuel and Charisma.

You can also check out the Outrageous Hope podcast on Spotify and Google Podcasts.

A Space for Your Own Notes
and Thoughts